THE
WILD
FLAG

E. B. WHITE

THE
WILD
FLAG

Editorials from
THE NEW YORKER
on Federal World Government
and Other Matters

HOUGHTON MIFFLIN COMPANY BOSTON
The Riverside Press Cambridge

ETGWt

4/11/46 Personnel #3↓

The Riverside Press
CAMBRIDGE · MASSACHUSETTS
PRINTED IN THE U.S.A.

ACKNOWLEDGMENT

THE EDITORIALS in this book were first published in *The New Yorker*. A few paragraphs of the Preface are taken from an article by E. B. White in *Transatlantic*, published in England by Penguin Books, Ltd., with the collaboration of the Writers' War Board.

PREFACE

THESE EDITORIALS appeared first in *The New Yorker*, on the page of notes and comment to which I occasionally contribute. I sign my name to them hesitantly, for it is questionable whether anyone can properly assume authorship of material which was published anonymously. An editorial writer refers to himself as 'we,' but is never sure who the other half of the 'we' is. I have yet to encounter the other half of 'we,' but expect to nail him in an alley some day and beat his brains out, to see what sort of stuffing is behind such omniscience.

Most publications, I think, make rather hard demands on their editorial writers, asking them to be consistent and sensible. *The New Yorker* has never suggested anything of the kind, and thus has greatly eased a writer's burden — for it is easier to say what you think if you don't feel obliged to follow a green arrow. *The New*

Yorker is both aloof and friendly toward its opinionated contributors, and I am grateful for this. I am reasonably sure that if some trusty around the place were to submit an editorial demanding that the George Washington Bridge be moved sixty feet further upstream and thatched with straw, the editors would publish it, no questions asked. This makes working for *The New Yorker* a unique pleasure — without, of course, explaining the other half of 'we.'

A recurrent theme of the book is world government, as distinct from the sort of international league which is now functioning under the name 'United Nations.' The most persistent criticism of world government is this: that although it may be a laudable idea, to discuss it is futile, even harmful, since there is no means of achieving it at present. This criticism may be valid. Certainly nobody, not even an editorial writer, can quite figure out how a world government could be set up when two of the biggest nations are operating under political systems which seem irreconcilable. But I believe that the case for a unified world is worth stating theoretically at any time. The answer to war is no war. And the likeliest means of removing war from the routine of national life is to elevate the community's authority to a level which is above national level. This, in fact, is the destination toward which the human race seems to be drifting, in violence and in pain; it should also be the goal toward which our statesmen are pointing, and I am afraid it seldom is. Much of the political construction which is being carried on in the name of humanity is still strictly limited to the national conception of human affairs. The first thing a draftsman does, when he prepares a charter, is to lock his country's sovereignty up in the safe so that nobody can tamper with it.

Nationalism is young and strong, and has already run into bad trouble. We take pains to educate our children at an early age in the rituals and mysteries of the nation, infusing national feeling into them in place of the universal feeling which is their birthright; but lately the most conspicuous activity of nations has been the blowing of each other up, and an observant child might reasonably ask whether he is pledging allegiance to a flag or to a shroud. A nation asks of its citizens everything — their fealty, their money, their faith, their time, their lives. It is fair to ask whether the nation, in return, does indeed any longer serve the best interests of the human beings who give so lavishly of their affections and their blood. We know, we Americans, what America means in the human heart; we remember its principles and we honor its record; but we tend to forget that it has its counterpart in sixty or seventy other places. This is mischievous business. It is bloody business. Reinforced with the atom, it may be fatal business.

Whether we wish it or not, we may soon have to make a clear choice between the special nation to which we pledge our allegiance and the broad humanity of which we are born a part. This choice is implicit in the world to come. We have a little time in which we can make the choice intelligently. Failing that, the choice will be made for us in the confusion of war, from which the world will emerge unified — the unity of total desolation.

The anatomy of loyalty is largely unexplored. Yet it is a branch of social science which suggests exciting discoveries for the long future. If the range of our planes continues to increase, the range of our thoughts will have to increase or there will be none of us left to do the thinking, and the focus of our allegiance will have to shift or we will find ourselves at last with nothing left to be loyal to. A world government, were we ever to get one, would impose on the individual the curious burden of taking the entire globe to his bosom — although not in any sense depriving him of the love of his front yard. The special feeling of an Englishman for a stream in Devonshire or a lane in Kent would have to run parallel to his pride in Athens and his insane love of Jersey City. The special feeling of a Netherlander for a dyke in Holland would have to extend onward and outward until it found the Norris Dam and the terraces of Egypt. A Chinese farmer in a rice paddy would have to feel, between his toes, not only the immediate wetness of his own field, but the vast wetness of the fertile world. A world made one, by the political union of its parts, would not only require of its citizen a shift of allegiance, but it would deprive him of the enormous personal satisfaction of distrusting what he doesn't know and despising what he has never seen. This would be a severe deprivation, perhaps an intolerable one. The awful truth is, a world government would lack an enemy, and that is a deficiency not to be lightly dismissed. It will take a yet undiscovered vitamin to supply the blood of man with a substitute for national ambition and racial antipathy; but we are discovering new vitamins all the time, and I am aware of that, too.

Two things in the human scene give encouragement to anyone who takes to brooding on these matters. For one thing, a cosmopolis is a fairly common sight. A big city is a noisy proof of man's ability to live at peace with strangers, with newcomers, and with what he blithely calls the 'objectionable elements.' The City of New York is a world government on a small scale. There, truly, is the world in a nutshell, its citizens meeting in the subway and ballpark, sunning on the benches in the square. They shove each other, but seldom too hard. They annoy each other, but rarely to the point of real trouble. There Greek and German work and pray, there Pole and Russian eat and dance. They enjoy the peace that goes with government, and the police are beautiful to behold. Any big city should be an important exhibit in the laboratory where the anatomy of loyalty is under investigation — and we had better not delay, either, for big cities are not as numerous as they were a few years ago. Some of them have turned up missing.

The other encouraging thing is that war is becoming increasingly unpopular with warriors. We needn't set too much store by this; nevertheless, it is stimulating to learn that the ones who have been doing the fighting have an extremely low opinion of the whole business. If war were only mildly unpopular, one might despair of ever getting rid of it down the drain. But war has reached a new low in the esteem of all people. The bombing of cities has made every civilian a participant in war, and this has swelled the ranks of war's detractors.

As for these editorials, they were written sometimes in anger and always in haste. They will be too purely theoretical for the practicing statesman, who is faced with the grim job of operating with equipment at hand, and too sweetly reasonable for the skeptic, who knows what an unpredictable customer the human being is. (A worker in the next stall has just informed me that world government is impractical because 'there are too many Orientals.') But theory and sweet reason are all right in their place; and if these topical paragraphs add an ounce to the long-continuing discussion of nationalism, and throw even as much as a flashlight's gleam on the wild flag which our children, and their children, must learn to know and love, I am satisfied.

E. B. W.

THE
WILD
FLAG

THE TIME is at hand to revive the discussion of companionate marriage, for it is now apparent that the passion of nations will shortly lead to some sort of connubial relationship, either a companionate one (as in the past) or a lawful one (which would be something new). If you observe closely the courtship among nations, if you read each morning the many protestations of affection and the lively plans for consummation, you will find signs that the drift is still toward an illicit arrangement based on love, respect, and a strong foreign policy. Countries appear to be on the verge of making new and solemn compacts with each other, of renewing old pledges. If it is to be this and no more, we predict that they will lie together in rapture for a while and then bust up as usual. The companionate idea is appealing to nations because it is familiar, because it demands little, and because it is exciting to the blood. The mention of a license and the thought of relinquishing something of one's independence come hard to the sovereign ear and mind. Even at this woebegone time it seems questionable whether the grim institution of marriage will be embraced by the world's states, which have always practiced free love and are used to its excesses and its tragic violence.

Our advice to the nations who call themselves united is to go out and buy rings. If there is to be love-in-bloom at the war's end, we should prefer to see it legal this time, if only for a change. The history of the modern world is the story of nations having affairs with each other. These affairs have been based on caprice and on ambition; they have been oiled with diplomacy and intrigue and have been unsanctified by law, there having been no law covering the rights and obligations of the contracting parties. The result has been chaotic and there still is no law. We are informed, almost hourly, that a new world order is in the making, yet most of the talk is of policy and almost none of the talk is of law.

America and China are in love. England and Russia are seen frequently together in public. France, Norway, the Netherlands, Greece, Poland, Czechoslovakia — each is groping for the other's hand in the darkness of the newsreel. What is going to come of this romantic and wonderful condition — a few stolen kisses, a key to an apartment somewhere, a renewal of individual vows and general irresponsibility? Considering how eager the nations are to lie down with each other, it seems to us time for a brief notice to be inserted in the world's paper, inviting interested parties to a preliminary meeting, a sociable if you want, to talk over the whole situation and perhaps even discuss the end of policy and laxity in their love life and the beginning of law and of force. The notice should be carefully worded and should be at least as honest as those wistful little ads which the lovelorn and the lonely place in the classified columns. It should conclude with that desperate yet somehow very hopeful phrase 'Object, matrimony.'

May 1, 1943

THE D.A.R., which has an enviable record of consistency, has adopted a resolution opposing any political union of the United States with other nations that would deprive this government of free and independent action. We commend to the Daughters the recent remarks of President Roosevelt at Monterrey on the subject of 'interdependence,' the word with the big new syllable.

The D.A.R. has also admonished its members to be on their guard against all proposals which might destroy the sovereignty of the American people. We commend to the Daughters the chapter on sovereignty in *A Democratic Manifesto*, which is the best book on the war and which shows sovereignty up for a dead cat.

The D.A.R. has further resolved that the main objective of the American people is to be victorious in the briefest possible time to prevent needless sacrifice of life. That just isn't true, for the people are obviously concerned with something beyond the mere negative ideal of Not Dying. That's three strikes on the Daughters of the American Revolution, who are swinging wide at the fast-breaking curves of war. Ladies, you're out!

DURING the great storm which broke following the announcement of the Jap executions of American fliers, two phrases were heard above the crackling fury of everyone's wrath: the Japs had 'violated military law' and the Japs would be 'brought to justice.' Now the storm abates. It is the time, now, for remembering that such phrases are false, such words dangerous when misused. The Japs violated no law and their leaders will never be brought to justice, though they will be brought to something else. Law is, unfortunately, not law unless it is enforceable, and the 'laws' of warfare are in their very nature unenforceable, being a mere set of rules for quarreling, which any country can disregard if it chooses. When war comes, each nation makes its own rules to suit itself. Japan makes hers, which include murdering enemy fliers; we make ours, which include abiding by previous agreements. When at length Japan is punished, as she certainly will be, for having executed American aviators, the act of punishing her will not be 'justice,' since no court exists which has jurisdiction and no force exists for carrying out such a court's order. To call it justice is to do ourselves a disservice, because it deflects our gaze from the terrible spectacle of a world without law.

This cantankerous attitude which we seem to be striking, this harping on the meaning of words, comes from our belief that there is a sharp need for definitions and that, in the words of Saroyan's barfly, there is 'no foundation all the way down the line.' Nothing is more frightening than to hear what is not law called law, what is not justice called justice. The recent murders in Japan, which received enormous public attention, were the inevitable extension of certain other Axis murders ten or twelve years ago, which received almost no attention. To speak as though we had law when what we've got is treaties and pacts, to use the word 'law' for non-law, is to lessen our chances of ever getting law among peoples, since the first step toward getting it is to realize, with dazzling clearness, that we haven't got it and never have had it.

Doctor Gallup, the asker, has asked people whether they favor an international police force, and three out of four have said they do. That is very nice. It is also quite misleading. Asking a man whether he wants an international police force is like asking him whether he wants the Rockettes. Of course he does, but the question is not whether he thinks the Rockettes are a good idea but whether he knows what is in back of them, making them effective; in short, whether he is in earnest about the girls and willing to give up time and money to build a stage big enough to hold them, hire an orchestra loud enough to accompany them, buy costumes rich enough to adorn them, and in general sustain an organization orderly enough to give them meaning and make them click. Doctor Gallup should ask his question again, this time adding, 'And you people realize, of course, that a police force is no good if simply used as a threat to strengthen agreements between independent powers, that to have meaning it must be the certified agent of the law, that to have law we must first have a constitutional world society, and that to achieve that each nation must say good-bye to its own freedom of action and to its long-established custom of doing as it damn well pleases. *Now* how many of you want an international police force?'

Here's one hand up, Doctor Gallup.

IT has been a long time since we have seen so many sensible remarks strung together as in the article by ex-Governor Stassen of Minnesota in last week's *Saturday Evening Post*. The author, who is now in the Navy, stated the case for world government in phrases which seemed to us clear, elevated, and sensible.

One of the curious difficulties in the way of world federation is the necessity of developing a planetary loyalty as a substitute for, or a complement to, national loyalty. In the United Nations of the World there will be no foreigner to make fun of, no outsider to feel better than. A citizen of the U.N.W. must take pride in the whole world; that, for some people, is going to be a very large thing to get excited about. A man will have to pledge allegiance not only to a national flag but to a universal banner, the colors of which will be rather unfamiliar. It is going to be a slow process, and the sooner we begin the better. The thing which would make it much easier, of course, would be if another planet should turn up as a rival for stratospheric power. If somebody were to discover rubber plantations on Mars, a world government would not only be a prime necessity, it would be a damn cinch.

Doctor Brickner, the psychiatrist, may
have diagnosed Germany's illness satisfactorily in his book *Is Germany Incurable?*, but he asked the wrong question. The
question is not whether the paranoid Germany is incurable but whether we are. All
Germany did was start a war; we and our
Allies have to finish one and then construct
a world out of broken promises and old
bottle caps. For this we need excellent
health and good vision. The odd thing
about paranoia is, you take a good look at
the patient and you can hardly tell it from
a real bad case of nationalism. Whatever
name you want to pin on Germany's trouble, it is contagious, it is human, and there
is a lot of it around. Doctor Brickner has
managed to give the impression that the
problem of the peace is a problem of turning Germans into nice people. This is misleading and gives many persons the same
sort of holier-than-thou feeling which Nazism celebrates. The question today is not
whether Germany is incurably paranoid
but whether her enemies are incurably
nationalistic. The answer to this question

is yet to be made and we advise our readers to keep their eye on the ball.

To a psychiatrist the world is likely to seem like a problem in psychiatry. Maybe it is, but we still think that the matter of arranging a suitable peace is a matter of extending the familiar technique by which human beings maintain order at city, state, and national levels to another level, at which they now merely dream of order. Paranoia is a relatively simple problem in communities which enjoy police, laws, courts, jails, hospitals, and doctors. It becomes unmanageable only at the global level, where none of these conveniences exists as yet.

IT IS already apparent that the word 'Fascist' will be one of the hardest-worked words in the Presidential campaign. Henry Wallace called some people Fascists the other day in a speech and next day up jumped Harrison Spangler, the Republican, to remark that if there were any Fascists in this country you would find them in the New Deal's palace guard. It is getting so a Fascist is a man who votes the other way. Persons who vote *your* way, of course, continue to be 'right-minded people.'

We are sorry to see this misuse of the word 'Fascist.' If we recall matters, a Fascist is a member of the Fascist party or a believer in Fascist ideals. These are: a nation founded on bloodlines, political expansion by surprise and war, murder or detention of unbelievers, transcendence of state over individual, obedience to one leader, contempt for parliamentary forms, plus some miscellaneous gymnastics for the young and a general feeling of elation. It seems to us that there are many New Deal Democrats who do not subscribe to such a program, also many aspiring Republicans. Other millions of Americans are nonsubscribers. It's too bad to emasculate the word 'Fascist' by using it on persons whose only offense is that they vote the wrong ticket. The word should be saved for use in cases where it applies, as it does to members of our Ku Klux Klan, for instance, whose beliefs and practices are identical with Fascism.

Unfortunately (or perhaps fortunately), there is a certain quality in Fascism which is quite close to a certain quality in nationalism. Fascism is openly against people-in-general, in favor of people-in-particular. Nationalism, although in theory not dedicated to such an idea, actually works against people-in-general because of its preoccupation with people-in-particular. It reminds one of Fascism, also, in its determination to stabilize its own position by whatever haphazard means present themselves — by treaties, policies, balances, agreements, pacts, and the jockeying for position which is summed up in the term 'diplomacy.' This doesn't make an America Firster a Fascist. It simply makes him, in our opinion, a man who hasn't grown into his pants yet. The persons who have written most persuasively against nationalism are the young soldiers who have got far enough from our shores to see the amazing implications of a planet. Once you see it, you never forget it.

Except for the food conference, the United Nations have maintained a physical aloofness which is lamentable and unpropitious. Time flashes by, or marches on, and still there are no United Nations in operation save as a remotely controlled coalition of fighting forces. This aloofness does not suggest a continuance of unity. It does not substantiate President Roosevelt's remark to the Canadian Parliament, 'There is a longing in the air . . . '

The essence of the spirit of community is a willingness to meet, whether in a grange hall, a town hall, a marble hall, or a hall bedroom. We see no possible excuse for delaying any longer the corporeality of the U.N. of the W. We respectfully recommend that a meeting be held in early fall, to be known as Meeting Number One, at which a chairman *pro tem* shall be elected, a resolution passed against members leaving their rubbers in the downstairs hall, and a motion made to adjourn, *sine die* and *sine odio,* to the World Series.

THE PACIFIC OCEAN, said Clarence Budington Kelland firmly, must become an American lake. He didn't make it clear why it should become an American lake rather than, say, a Chinese lake or a Russian lake. The Chinese were seaside dwellers along the Pacific many thousands of years before the Americans, and presumably even now like to gaze upon its blue and sometimes tranquil waters. This may seem annoying to a party leader, who is apt to find it difficult to believe that there can be anybody of any importance on the far end of a lake. Yet the Pacific and its subsidiary seas are presumably real and agreeable to the people who live on them. The Sea of Okhotsk is five times the size of Mr. Kelland's state of Arizona, the Sea of Japan is longer than the longest serial he ever wrote, the Yellow Sea is as big as the Paramount Building and bigger, and the South China Sea runs on endlessly into the sunset beyond Borneo. Are these the coves in an American lake — little bays where we can go to catch our pickerel among the weeds?

To the twenty-nine members of the House of Representatives who voted against the Fulbright resolution, who fear entanglement with other nations, and who would preserve all our sovereignty and independence; to these twenty-nine unforgettable legislators whose dim, aloof spirit walks by its wild lone, we now award a special ribbon for unusual density above and beyond the call of duty. The ribbon is made of bloody bandages, and we hope it will forever remind the representatives of the real entanglements of the flesh which belie their quaint and curious theory. Gentlemen, if you do not know that your country is now entangled beyond recall with the rest of the world, what *do* you know?

This is the dream we had, asleep in our chair, thinking of Christmas in lands of the fir tree and pine, Christmas in lands of the palm tree and vine, and of how the one great sky does for all places and all people.

After the third war was over (this was our curious dream), there was no more than a handful of people left alive, and the earth was in ruins and the ruins were horrible to behold. The people, the survivors, decided to meet to talk over their problem and to make a lasting peace, which is the customary thing to make after a long, exhausting war. There were eighty-three countries, and each country sent a delegate to the convention. One Englishman came, one Peruvian, one Ethiopian, one Frenchman, one Japanese, and so on, until every country was represented. Each delegate brought the flag of his homeland with him — each, that is, except the delegate from China. When the others asked him why he had failed to bring a flag, he said that he had discussed the matter with another Chinese survivor, an ancient and very wise man, and that between them they had concluded that they would not have any cloth flag for China any more.

'What kind of flag *do* you intend to have?' asked the delegate from Luxembourg.

The Chinese delegate blinked his eyes and produced a shoebox, from which he drew a living flower which looked very like an iris.

'What is that?' they all inquired, pleased with the sight of so delicate a symbol.

'That,' said the Chinese, 'is a wild flag, *Iris tectorum*. In China we have decided to adopt this flag, since it is a convenient and universal device and very beautiful and grows everywhere in the moist places of the earth for all to observe and wonder at. I propose all countries adopt it, so that it will be impossible for us to insult each other's flag.'

'Can it be waved?' asked the American delegate, who wore a troubled expression and a Taft button.

The Chinese gentleman moved the flag gently to and fro. 'It can be waved, yes,' he answered. 'But it is more interesting in repose or as the breeze stirs it.'

[21]

'I see it is monocotyledonous,' said the Dutch delegate, who was an amiable man.

'I don't see how a strong foreign policy can be built around a wild flag which is the same for everybody,' complained the Latvian.

'It can't be,' said the Chinese. 'That is one of the virtues of my little flag. I should remind you that the flag was once yours, too. It is the oldest flag in the world, the original one, you might say. We are now, gentlemen, in an original condition again. There are very few of us.'

The German delegate arose stiffly. 'I would be a poor man indeed,' he said, 'did I not feel that I belonged to the master race. And for that I need a special flag, *natürlich*.'

'At the moment,' replied the Chinaman, 'the master race, like so many other races, is suffering from the handicap of being virtually extinct. There are fewer than two hundred people left in the entire world, and we suffer from a multiplicity of banners.'

The delegate from Patagonia spoke up.

'I fear that the wild flag, one for all, will prove an unpopular idea.'

'It will, undoubtedly,' sighed the Chinese delegate. 'But now that there are only a couple of hundred people on earth, even the word "unpopular" loses most of its meaning. At this juncture we might conceivably act in a sensible, rather than a popular, manner.' And he produced eighty-two more shoeboxes and handed a wild flag to each delegate, bowing ceremoniously.

Next day the convention broke up and the delegates returned to their homes, marveling at what they had accomplished in so short a time. And that is the end of our dream.

A VOICE from our radio buttonholed us the other evening and issued a sharp warning. Russia, said the voice, is obviously out for all she can get. England is obviously trying to regain her empire and beat us to trade routes. If we know what's good for us, we will accept the challenge and enter the race. What we need is a clear, well-defined foreign policy based on self-interest.

This voice, so worldly wise, so shrewd, has encouraged us to formulate just such a foreign policy for the United States. We are a believer in self-interest. In order, however, that our suggested policy be clear and carefully defined, we shall have to pause for a moment to inquire into the meaning and nature of policy itself.

Policy is a system of conduct shaped by expediency. It is supported by diplomacy and it takes for granted independence of action. Because of its peculiar nature, policy is a luxury which the world can probably no longer afford, although the world realizes this only dimly and may not perceive it sharply for many years to come.

Walter Lippmann has written a book on the subject of foreign policy, defining it as the 'shield of the republic' — an accurate term, the shield being a traditional device in war and war being the clash of two or more policies. It is impossible to envision an orderly world in which policy remains the accepted instrument of government and in which sixty or seventy nations each arrive independently at a clear, well-defined foreign policy based on self-interest. Such a political arrangement is essentially chaotic, and will remain so, in our opinion. It is as though eighteen ball players went out on a diamond, each having evolved his own policy regarding the bat, the ball, the glove, and the bases. One player's policy is to run directly from first to third without bothering with second. Another secretly resolves to conceal a bat in his shirt and rap the pitcher over the head with it. Another decides to keep tossing the ball up in the air and catching it, in solitary glee. It doesn't make for an orderly ball game, yet it is the system by which nations live and it is the principle

[25]

which our radio voice advises us to perpetuate.

Where written law governs people's actions (that is, in the city, in the state, in the nation), the individual does not enjoy the privilege of policy and does not expect to. He enjoys, instead, the protection of codified morality and the dull, pleasant society of lawyers and cops. Yet this individual, who has himself long since surrendered the privilege of policy, still insists that his country shall exercise it. This is an absurd situation, which is slowly drawing to a logical climax in the bombed cities and in the terrible, bloody jungles. The question the war has raised, higher than a jet plane, is whether nations can continue to exist by policy.

In the absence of constitutional world law, in the absence of government on a planetary level, a nation has no alternative but to find a policy and pursue it. The United States is no exception. Mr. Lippmann, in his book, suggests that our foreign policy be to cultivate the right people — which is as flimsy a program for a nation as for an individual. Such a foreign policy is not only a shield of the republic, it is practically an admission that the republic will again have to use the shield in battle. Therefore, we shall now suggest a somewhat more difficult policy. To us it seems clear and well defined. It is, in short, the only decent course for a nation to follow. We propose that *it shall be the policy of the United States to bring to an end the use of policy*.

No other policy will lead us toward peace. No other makes any sense in the long run. No other is in our self-interest, no matter how advantageous to us it may appear to be.

Lord Cranborne pointed out last week that when the Allies meet to reconstruct the Atlantic Charter, the fixing would be done by the powers. Small nations, he said, would not be included in the talks because to include them would be to 'cause confusion.' Seems very probable it would. Complications are bound to arise when you consult *all* the interested parties in any affair. Nevertheless, we strongly recommend this sort of confusion. There are really two types of confusion which should be recognized nowadays — there is the confusion of representation (which is a rather hopeful and honest confusion), and there is the confusion of exclusion (which is a familiar system of trouble and which has brought us to the utter confusion of the past three or four years). The powers would like to avoid the embarrassment of having to compose a global document in the presence of others. But if a big nation finds it confusing to write a charter when little nations are in the room, imagine the confusion a little nation feels reading a finished document it has never even seen a draft of.

A V-MAIL LETTER from a sergeant in New Guinea asks us to help him and other soldiers form an opinion of the Presidential candidates. 'Make it possible for us to study an unbiased presentation of the records of the candidates,' he writes.

We've been digging around in our desk to see what records we possess. Most of them don't throw any light, and none is unbiased. At the moment the only presentable material at hand is something Dewey said at Mackinac and something Stassen wrote for the *Saturday Evening Post.*

Subject: The postwar world.

Dewey: '... the United States must be prepared to undertake new obligations and responsibilities in the community of nations. We must co-operate with other nations to promote the wider international exchange of goods and services, to broaden access to raw materials, to achieve monetary and economic stability, and thus discourage the growth of rampant nationalism and its spawn, economic and military aggression.'

[29]

Stassen: '. . . whenever men are living close together they need a government to prevent anarchy and conflict, and to permit progress. The news we read and hear each day clearly indicates that government limited to the national level will not be enough in the years ahead. Nor will treaties, pacts, and agreements between nations meet the need. The nations of the world must not merely agree that they wish to live together in peace; they must establish a mechanism of government to achieve this end.'

We present these two utterances for what they are worth to a voter in New Guinea. Our advice to soldier voters is to watch for candidates who can pronounce the word 'government' without flinching and who don't call it 'co-operation' or confuse the two things.

WE RECEIVED a letter from the Writers' War Board the other day asking for a statement on 'The Meaning of Democracy.' It presumably is our duty to comply with such a request, and it is certainly our pleasure.

Surely the Board knows what democracy is. It is the line that forms on the right. It is the don't in Don't Shove. It is the hole in the stuffed shirt through which the sawdust slowly trickles; it is the dent in the high hat. Democracy is the recurrent suspicion that more than half of the people are right more than half of the time. It is the feeling of privacy in the voting booths, the feeling of communion in the libraries, the feeling of vitality everywhere. Democracy is the score at the beginning of the ninth. It is an idea which hasn't been disproved yet, a song the words of which have not gone bad. It's the mustard on the hot dog and the cream in the rationed coffee. Democracy is a request from a War Board, in the middle of a morning in the middle of a war, wanting to know what democracy is.

PEACE through supremacy seems to be one of the more popular peace devices. 'We must win the peace by assuring the continuation of America's supremacy in the air,' said Colonel N. Jay Boots the other day. 'Common sense,' said Alexander de Seversky, 'indicates that we shall require air power superior to that of any potential enemy or group of enemies.' In short, be supreme. The advice is offered by a formidable group of thinkers, and it reminds us of that charming bit of Gilbertian advice: 'Oh, be Early English, ere it is too late!' The thing we find hard to understand about supremacy is why, if it is right for America, it isn't right for every other nation. If it's sensible for Americans to establish American supremacy, surely it is sensible for, oh, let's say Russians, to establish Russian supremacy. Or for Guatemalans to establish Guatemalan supremacy. Yet if Russia were to announce that 'common sense indicates' that peace could be attained only through Russian air supremacy, Colonel Boots would be fit to be

[32]

tied. One nation's common sense is another nation's high blood pressure.

Our advice for winning the peace is not to establish supremacy in the air but to establish political union on the ground.

Behold the platform speaker! He grasps the microphone as coolly as though it were a broom handle in his mother's kitchen and warns you (a thousand miles away) to beware of fantastic schemes. Standing there, speaking in a natural tone of voice, he is of the very nature of fantasy. His words leap across rivers and mountains, but his thoughts are still only six inches long.

We have received ample assurance from practical politicians that a federalized world is preposterous and fantastic. But we also have been assured that the short range of the present rocket bombs will soon be corrected. Every day the importance of being fantastic becomes clearer. It does not seem a bit too fantastic to us that the people of this small world should indulge themselves in a common government, or that a Britisher, a Portuguese, and a Hollander should live under the same bill of rights.

The men of Dumbarton Oaks are hunched over their U-shaped table as we write this. We wish them strength, wisdom, vision. Specifically, we wish them the strength to be fantastic. If they arise from their table with a diagram that is less fantastic, we'll say, than a radio set or a rocket bomb, then they will have failed and we shall have been betrayed. Of what use is it to equip our ships with the most sensitive detection devices, so they can hear faint vibrations at great distances, only to entrust our lives and fortunes to the deaf, who can't even hear the vibrations of a kettledrum in the same room with them? We wish the conferees strength, wisdom, vision, keen hearing. There are universal vibrations that must be picked up at just this moment in history. They are as insistent as insects in the grass.

Everybody likes to hear about a man laying down his life for his country, but nobody wants to hear about a country giving her shirt for her planet. Why is that? You would think that after such a demonstration of self-sacrifice as we have seen, any nation would gladly bleed and die for the world. Who are we to play the peace safe? After such deeds.

Query: What does Mr. Hull mean when

he speaks of 'all peace-loving nations'? Who is to decide what nation is peace-loving, what nation war-loving? Germany and Japan, by their own definition, are peace-loving nations, engaged in establishing world peace according to their lights. To many Finns, Russia must seem a war-loving nation. Is Italy a peace-loving or a war-loving nation? It depends on whether you're talking about Italy in the first World War, when she was on our side, or in the second World War, when she was on the other. We will never get anywhere till we stop talking about 'all peace-loving nations.' The phrase is 'all nations.'

Sir Alexander Cadogan, head of the British group at the conference, said that 'the nations of the world should maintain, according to their capacities, sufficient forces available for joint action when necessary to prevent breaches of the peace.' A good point. A good point but an old story. The peace of the world was breached when Fascism began to spread its crimes against society in the nineteen-twenties, but although there was at that time among the nations of the world plenty of force available to prevent the breach, there was no tendency toward joint action. Nor will there be any tendency toward joint action as long as the world is run on the principle of national sovereignty, by a system of agreements between sovereign nations. There will never be any tendency toward joint action until it is too late. Therefore, the problem is not how to make force available for joint action but how to make world government available so that action won't have to be joint.

THE Department of Agriculture has sent us a list of the achievements of its scientists during recent years. It is a list that makes one proud. A cork substitute, a phosphate drink for cattle, a louse powder for the armed forces, a small turkey, starch from sweet potatoes, lacquer from cow's milk, tannin from sumac, a new method of dehydrating cheese, a new poison bait for the Mormon cricket, a preservative for chicken feathers, a smear for screw-worms, a hybrid onion, and a design for a hydraulic drop structure for gully control. Such tangible evidence of human ingenuity and perseverance should be an inspiration to our statesmen, who are still fumbling among their test tubes for a substitute for war and a smear for tyrants in the larval stage. The world, gentlemen, is your laboratory, and please don't blow us all up trying to develop a preservative for national sovereignty. You've fooled with that one long enough.

Pᴿᴱˢᴵᴰᴱᴺᵀ Rᴏᴏˢᴇᴠᴇʟᴛ reported that the Dumbarton Oaks people had agreed on ninety per cent of the problems before them. There was non-agreement, he said, on only ten per cent. This ten per cent of non-agreement, according to the Associated Press, 'is understood to be primarily on the question of whether a powerful nation can veto international action against itself.' But that, of course, isn't ten per cent; it is about 99.44 per cent. It is, specifically, the question of sovereignty, which makes everyone gulp, as well it might. A league of sovereign, independent nations faces a problem of police control which is insoluble. It may define aggression, draw rules, and agree on a means of enforcing the rules, but it still must founder on the ledge of sovereignty and on the test of whether, in a pinch, a nation shall control its own destiny and act as it pleases. If you like, you may call this ten per cent, but at a place like Munich (which is where it lands you eventually) it looks bigger than that, and tougher.

THE NAME of the new peace organization is to be the United Nations. It is a misnomer and will mislead the people. The name of the organization should be the League of Free and Independent Nations Pledged to Enforce Peace, or the Fifty Sovereign Nations of the World Solemnly Sworn to Prevent Each Other from Committing Aggression. These titles are clumsy, candid, and damning. They are exact, however. The phrase 'United Nations' is inexact, because it implies union, and there is no union suggested or contemplated in the work of Dumbarton Oaks. The nations of the world league will be united only as fifty marbles in a dish are united. Put your toe on the dish and the marbles will scatter, each to its own corner.

Wendell Willkie knew that a league of free countries is not a world government of united nations. He saw this and preached unity — sometimes in a rather confused manner but with conviction and often with luster. His great phrase 'One World' is his monument. His book wasn't a very good book, but it was an important

[40]

book and will take its place on the permanent shelf of this groping, hopeful planet. Willkie understood that the price of world order is national sovereignty, and he dared say so right to his party's face. Before he died he accused both parties of holding out the false promise that 'permanent or lasting peace can be attained without what is popularly called "loss of sovereignty."' Where is the Republican or the Democrat who will take up from there?

A security league to keep the peace is a negative project and follows a negative pattern. Peace is not something to be kept, like a pet monkey; peace is the by-product of responsible government. The league of Dumbarton Oaks is already revealing its irresponsible character by designating some nations 'peace-loving,' some nations 'big' — as though we all enjoyed the services of a referee. But the league of Dumbarton Oaks, whatever we may think of it, is what we are to live with for a while. It is the symbol of our honorable intentions and the legitimate child of our delegated authority. It is the sort of temporary structure you see at a world's fair, made of

[41]

wallboard and fireproof shingles, and there is nothing to stop us from dismantling it at any time and building something solid. These are great days, when anything can happen. Now, as Tom Paine said, is the seed-time of union.

A first step to prepare a seed-bed would be for believers in world government (and there are many groups in many countries) to close their ranks. Unless they themselves can unite, which should be a fairly simple task, they can hardly expect their nations to unite, which would be at best a very complicated one. Therefore we say, 'Federalists of the world, unite!'

The more a man thinks about it, the more clearly he sees that the political world must keep pace with the scientific world. A security league, in an age of flight, is an anomaly. Politically the shape of the new world must be the shape of penicillin and sulfa and blood plasma, the shape of the buzz bomb and the V-2 and the X-903, the shape of the mothproof closet and the shatter-proof glass and the helicopter with the built-in waffle iron. This is a shape to conjure with. Mr. Willkie gave us the design in two words. If we try to live with all these majestic and fantastic and destructive gifts of science in a political framework reminiscent of the one-hoss shay, in danger of being upset by the irresponsibilities of diplomacy and the delicate balances of regional alliances and the wistful vetoes of the accused, we will soon enough discover disaster. There is good reason to believe that if statecraft is again caught lagging ten jumps behind science, we will never crawl back to life again as we have done this time. What curious defect it is in us that we should endorse the supercharger and deny the supra-state!

The peace of Dumbarton Oaks is the best our leading men could devise. It is an honest try; we must believe that. It is the work of the ripe, the middle-aged, the experienced, the practical, attempting to repair the damage caused by the war fought by the callow, the young, the inexperienced, the dreamers. We would like to hear from these veterans of battle, these neophytes of peace. We wonder how satisfied they are with the security of national alignments and friendly juxtapositions and solemn pledges that the good shall police the bad. To match this war we need a peace of magnificent proportions and un-dreamed-of design. We give only a hint: It must be in the shape of the letter 'O,' it must be in the shape of the terrestrial globes in the fifty separate state departments of the fifty separate nations called United.

THERE IS NOW a demand that Nazi leaders be 'tried and punished' for all
crimes back as far as 1933. Yet the cold
truth is there is not a Nazi living who can
be tried or brought to justice for anything
he has done, because we have no justice to
bring him to. To talk of justice as though
it were something you could pull out of a
hat, as occasion requires, is to talk idly and
badly. When a German officer tortures
and butchers the innocent people of a village, he can be caught and shot by a firing
squad (and we trust he will be), but he
cannot be brought to justice. The only
way you can try and punish an individual
who has committed an antisocial act on an
international level is by setting up shop
on that level, creating the courts on that
level, writing the laws on that level, and
supporting the enforcement on that level.
Whether people want to set up shop on
that level, whether people are capable of
it, whether it is wise to attempt it — these
are questions still unanswered by the democratic nations. Our private hope is that
the answer will be Yes, but until the peo-

ple make up their minds they ought to keep the record clean and not kid themselves about jurisdiction and crime. You can't have your anarchical society and eat it too.

One of the so-called crimes the Germans committed eleven years ago was the burning of the books in public — a universal gesture of contempt for the free circulation of human ideas. Such an act was incipient aggression and was on the level we've been talking about. Query: Does the world want a law prohibiting an individual from burning books in public? Query: Does it want a law prohibiting a fanatical German or a fanatical Anybody from murdering innocent villagers? Query: Does it want a law, applicable to all people, which says, 'Thou shalt not spit in thy neighbor's eye'? You can answer those questions any way you like, but you can't pretend that that sort of justice is here yet. The road leading to it is a long, tough one, and we haven't even started up it. The league structure proposed at Dumbarton Oaks does not seem to us to lead toward the goal (except in spirit), since a league is

[46]

a mere caricature of government, with nations attempting to judge nations and the individual left out of the picture. Our belief is that the way lies through a federation of democratic countries, which differs from a league in that it has a legislature that can legislate, a judiciary that can judge, and an executive that can execute. It does not have to operate through diplomacy, and it has a No Fooling sign on the door.

THEY are not wrapped as gifts (there was no time to wrap them), but you will find them under the lighted tree with the other presents. They are the extra gifts, the ones with the hard names. Certain towns and villages. Certain docks and installations. Atolls in a sea. Assorted airstrips, beachheads, supply dumps, rail junctions. Here is a gift to hold in your hand — Hill 660. Vital from a strategic standpoint. 'From the Marines,' the card says. Here is a small strip of the Italian coast. Merry Christmas from the members of the American Fifth (who waded ashore). This is Kwajalein, Maloelap, Wotje. This is Eniwetok. Place them with your other atolls, over by the knitted scarf from Aunt Lucy. Here is Gea. If the size isn't right, remember it was selected at night, in darkness. Roi, Mellu, Boggerlapp, Ennugarret, Ennumennet, Ennubirr. Amphibious forces send season's greetings. How pretty! A little reef-fringed islet in a coral sea. Kwajalein! A remembrance at Christmas from the Seventh Division. Los Negros Island. Put it with the others of the Admiralty Group. Elements of the First Cavalry Division (dismounted) have sent Momote airfield, a very useful present. Manus, largest of the Admiralties. Lorengau, taken from the Japanese garrison in the underground bunkers. Talasea airdrome. Wotho Atoll (a gift from the Twenty-Second Marine Regiment). Emirau Island, and ten more atolls in the Marshalls to make your Christmas bright in 1944: Ujae, Lae, Lib, Namu, Ailinglapalap (never mind the names), together with a hundred-and-fifty-mile strip of the northern New Guinea coast, Tanahmera Bay and Humboldt Bay, together with Hollandia. 'From some American troops covered with red mud.'

Here is a novel gift — a monastery on a hill. It seems to have been damaged. A bridge on Highway 6. A mountain stronghold, Castelforte (Little Cassino, they used to call it). And over here the roads — Via Casilina and the Appian Way. Valleys, plains, hills, roads, and the towns and villages. Santa Maria Infante, San Pietro, Monte Cerri, and Monte Bracchi. One reads the names on the cards with affection.

Best wishes from the Fifth. Gaeta, Cisterna, Terracina, the heights behind Velletri, the Alban Hills, Mount Peschio, and the fortress of Lazio. Velletri and Valmontone. Best wishes from the Fifth. The suburbs of Rome, and Rome. The Eternal City! Holiday greetings from the American Fifth.

Who wouldn't love the Norman coast for Christmas? Who hasn't hoped for the Atlantic Wall, the impregnable? Here is the whole thing under the lighted tree. First the beaches (greetings from the Navy and the Coast Guard), then the cliffs, the fields behind the cliffs, the inland villages and towns, the key places, the hedgerows, the lanes, the houses, and the barns. Ste. Mère Eglise (with greetings from Omar Bradley and foot soldiers). This Norman cliff (best from the Rangers). St. Jacques de Nehou (from the Eighty-Second Airborne Division, with its best). Cherbourg — street by street, and house by house. St. Remy des Landes, La Broquière, Baudreville, Neufmesnil, La Poterie, the railroad station at La Haye du Puits. And then St. Lô, and the whole vista of France.

When have we received such presents? Saipan in the Marianas — only they forgot to take the price tag off. Saipan cost 9752 in dead, wounded, and missing, but that includes a mountain called Tapotchau. Guam. 'Merry Christmas from Conolly, Geiger, and the boys.' Tinian, across the way. Avranches, Gavray, Torigny-sur-Vire, a German army in full retreat under your tree. A bridge at Pontorson, a bridge at Ducey, with regards from those who take bridges. Rennes, capital of Brittany (our columns fan out). Merry Christmas, all! Brest, Nantes, St. Malo, a strategic fortress defended for two weeks by a madman. Toulon, Nice, St. Tropez, Cannes (it is very gay, the Riviera, very fashionable). And now (but you must close your eyes for this one) . . . Paris.

Still the gifts come. You haven't even noticed the gift of the rivers Marne and Aisne. Château-Thierry, Soissons (this is where you came in). Verdun, Sedan (greetings from the American First Army, greetings from the sons of the fathers). Here is a most unusual gift, a bit of German soil. Priceless. A German village, Roetgen. A forest south of Aachen. Liége, the Belfort Gap, Geilenkirchen, Crucifix Hill, Uebach. Morotai Island in the Halmaheras. An airport on Peleliu. Angaur (from the Wildcats). Nijmegen Bridge, across the Rhine. Cecina, Monteverdi, more towns, more villages on the Tyrrhenian coast. Leghorn. And, as a special remembrance, sixty-two ships of the Japanese Navy, all yours. Tacloban, Dulag, San Pablo . . . Ormoc. Valleys and villages in the Burmese jungle. Gifts in incredible profusion and all unwrapped, from old and new friends: gifts with a made-in-China label, gifts from Russians, Poles, British, French, gifts from Eisenhower, de Gaulle, Montgomery, Malinovsky, an umbrella from the Air Forces, gifts from engineers, rear gunners, privates first class . . . there isn't time to look at them all. It will take years. This is a Christmas you will never forget, people have been so generous.

L AST WEEK when things were at a low point in Europe, we sat reading the paper, trying to figure out who was going to win — just a nervous little homebody in a sack suit, trying to unravel supply lines, spearheads, flank movements, reinforcements, armor, weather, and the whole impossible mystery of modern tactical warfare. We got mired, as any civilian does. But in the middle of this imbecile business our eye went over to a photograph on an inside page of the paper, and something about the picture stopped us cold. It was a little out of date, maybe, but it showed a couple of Yanks straightening up the inside of a synagogue in Holland which had been desecrated by Germans on an earlier visit. Here was the thing that has a way of getting forgotten in the middle of a war, and we were reminded, rather sharply, that there is an idea that travels with Allied armor and that it is neither a new idea nor one about which any American soldier or civilian need feel the slightest misgivings. Anyone who isn't sure who is going to win, those who would liberate the spirit or

[53]

those who would calcify it, had better quit fiddling with newspapers and armies. There is not much, at the moment, to indicate that 1945 will be a happy year, but for those who fight along with this main idea, whether in the glint of battle or in the uneasy chair of civil life, the year is already clothed in a certain historical radiance like that of stars of the first magnitude.

COMMISSIONER Moss, trying to distinguish between a show that is a hit and a show that isn't, reminded us of the people who are trying to distinguish between a country that is important and one that isn't. The Commissioner's plan, we note, was abandoned at last in favor of one in which all shows have the same status under the rules. State Department please copy.

IN HIS INAUGURAL ADDRESS, President Roosevelt said that we had learned to be citizens of the world, but he did not tell us where we might apply for our first papers. The world's department of justice is still a long subway ride from any given point, but to go forever unnaturalized, in so promising a land, is unthinkable.

Kent Cooper, an unnaturalized citizen of the world, spoke up the other day for a worldwide free press and for the people's 'right to know.' It seemed to us, reading his speech, that he didn't make clear that the right to know is inseparable from the willingness to be known. Like all rights, it is achieved only by the surrender of individual freedoms and immunities and by the assumption of civil obligations. A free world press is possible, we'd say, only as part of the structure of free world government, whose citizens, for the sake of gaining the right to know, relinquish the antique pleasure of remaining mutually unknowable; that is, detached, separate, independent.

Even within a political unit such as

ours, where a free press is fundamental to our society, the right to know stops abruptly at the threshold of the State Department. We have never, as citizens of a republic, enjoyed the right to know what goes on in that difficult region where national government ends and the international poker game begins. That being the case, our chances of achieving a worldwide free press appear to us only as good as our chances of achieving a federal world government. If the United Nations choose to unite in peace, we can reasonably expect a world press that is informative and untainted. If the United Nations choose to remain separate, isolated, and independent, if they revive diplomacy-as-usual, what global citizen is so naïve as to believe that he will have the 'right to know'? He not only won't have the right to know but he won't have a prayer of finding out. He can plant an A.P. correspondent at the door of every council chamber from here to there and back again, and he still won't find out.

In time of war, the State cuts deeply into the citizen's right to know. The State sits in the editor's chair and draws the editor's mantle close. A piece of fiction by a soldier came into this office the other day, and it had obviously been censored not only for reasons of security but for reasons of taste. The Army censor had not liked the way one of the characters talked, so he had removed some of the conversation. We get goose pimples when we feel the blue pencil being taken gently out of our hands. We wish to remind censors that it is a very old pencil. Somebody gave it to us in 1791, and we wouldn't lose it for anything.

A S VICTORY over Germany gets nearer, the spirits of everyone seem to go down, and anxieties increase. In the men's room, a fellow assures us that within ten years we will be at war with Russia. He has been in Russia. 'The picture is black, I see nothing but trouble.' In a doctor's office, the doctor (born in Vienna) tells us he is disturbed by the Yalta meeting. 'In gaining a military victory,' he says, 'we have suffered a diplomatic defeat of the first water.' (Germany should have been left strong, to keep the balance in Europe.) In a taxicab, the driver explains to us that Russia hates Catholics. 'There's a hundred and fifty million Cat'lics — nobody ain't gonna push *them* around.' In *Time,* a long article explains the 'stubborn facts' of the case. (Roosevelt and Churchill had to go wherever Stalin wanted to go.) In the morning mail, a long letter announces a scheme for resuscitating America after the 'complete collapse' and the 'four years of chaos' which will follow this war — a modern Noah, already banging away at his Ark.

France is worried about 'greatness.' Dakar must be fortified and improved so that the *greatness* of France will be reaffirmed. (As though we had not all lately been ill of the disease greatness, France most critically of all.) England is worried about America's head start in postwar aviation. Senator Vandenberg says we must make a 'hard and fast' treaty with all our Allies (as though a treaty could be anything but soft and fast). We debate at length whether we should have compulsory military training after the war, to provide a strong national defense (knowing perfectly well that no matter what sort of arms we maintain, other countries will set to work to match us man for man, gun for gun, invention for invention).

Delegates are appointed to travel to San Francisco in April to reshape this frightened world, this suspicious planet. The ex-Secretary of State. The Dean of Barnard. Some members of Congress. Commander Stassen. They will be asked to write a document to end trouble, to bring peace. They will speak enthusiastically of the 'family of nations.' Some are already making hasty notes on their cuff of weights, balances, potencies, impotencies, voting procedures, veto powers, and of whether Mr. Big can do this to Mr. Little. On Tuesday we have the Big Three. On Thursday we have the Big Five. On Sunday we have church, and the opportunity to pray.

The world, being now afraid of its own shadow, is ripe for something bigger than it seems likely to get, broader than it believes itself capable of achieving. If ever people needed to see clearly that their special national interests are identical with their special national decline, it is in these nervous times.

Three-quarters of a century ago, Renan wrote, 'The greatest fault that the liberal school could commit in the midst of the horrors besieging us would be to despair. The future belongs to her. The war, object of future maledictions, was possible because people sidestepped the liberal maxims which are at the same time those of peace and the union of peoples. . . . Events and the majority opinion give me the lie. Nevertheless, I cannot say that I am converted; let us wait ten or fifteen years.'

That was 1871.

An arresting fact about warfare is that it is now unpopular with the men who are engaged in it and with the people who are supporting it. Only a minority approve of the broad general business of armed slaughter and destruction. And if a thing is unpopular, there is always the amusing possibility that it may not, then, be inevitable.

The delegates to San Francisco have the most astonishing job that has ever been dumped into the laps of a few individuals. On what sort of rabbit they pull from the hat hang the lives of most of us, and of our sons and daughters. If they put on their spectacles and look down their noses and come up with the same old bunny, we shall very likely all hang separately — nation against nation, power against power, defense against defense, people (reluctantly) against people (reluctantly). If they manage to bring the United Nations out of the bag, full blown, with constitutional authority and a federal structure having popular meaning, popular backing, and an over-all authority greater than the authority of any one member or any combination of members, we might well be started up a new road.

The pattern of life is plain enough. The world shrinks. It will eventually be unified. What remains to be seen (through eyes that now bug out with mortal terror) is whether the last chapter will be written in blood or in Quink.

A SECURITY LEAGUE in which some nations may be coerced and other nations
may not does not recommend itself to the
logical mind, any more than does a club in
which some members may be spanked and
others may not. However good their intentions and strong their efforts, designers
of leagues run at last into this familiar
dilemma. They run into the stone face of
absolute nationalism, and into the impossible task of applying law and order to political entities. They run into the curious
little bug that lives in leagues, an inerad-
icable bug. This bug was in the old League
of Nations, and it turns up again, wiggling
its feelers, in this new proposal. A league
does not provide law and courts, because
a league insists on sovereignty, thus imply-
ing that a nation shall be its own law. A
league does not provide world government; it provides merely a new set of
promises, a new set of balances, a new expression of good faith.

At least one of our delegates to San
Francisco knows that the world is sorely
in need of government on a higher level.

Commander Stassen said the words last week. His speech in Minnesota was something new in political utterances, for it not only proposed a universal bill of rights but told what the cost of such a document would be. It was the first great speech on federal union which contained the price tag, and it shook our timbers.

'There may be many diplomats who do not know it, there may be many political leaders who are afraid to admit it, there may be people who do not understand it; but the extreme principle of absolute nationalistic sovereignty is of the Middle Ages and it is dead. . . . [1] True sovereignty rests in the people. . . .'

There are the words to keep and love, all you who fight abroad, all you who weep at home.

One thing about Stassen, he seems to want to find out what other people think about all this business. He went to see Governor Dewey to ask what he thought, and, whether because of encouragement

[1] The Commander used an unfortunate figure of speech. Several irate mediaevalists wrote in, pointing out that in the Middle Ages sovereignty did not reside mainly in national states.

or because of desperation, he beat it right from Albany to Cambridge to ask the Harvard faculty what *they* thought. That shows an open mind and a sense of direction. It also shows that he is afflicted with the awful loneliness that occasionally settles on a believer in one world. To give this planet even one basic law would require that a little swatch be snipped from everyone's flag and applied to the world's banner, and that, of course, is the most delicate and dangerous surgery ever proposed. Just thinking about it makes a man lonely — makes him want to run up to Harvard and ask Mom if it's all right.

≁

Children have the gift of solving things directly, easily, and sometimes brilliantly. They do not refer questions back to dubious standards, and they ignore precedents. Something happened recently in Germantown, Pennsylvania, which perfectly illustrates this peculiar gift — we heard of it through a friend. In Germantown there are two schools, one predominantly colored, one predominantly white. The gangs of little boys from the two schools often play together. One day they invented a new game called Race Riot, but when they got assembled to play it they discovered that there were more white boys than colored boys. Clearly the thing was out of balance and unfair. What to do? Like a flash the children had the answer. The proper number of white boys promptly volunteered to play colored, and the race riot proceeded with even numbers, in perfect equality. Adults, we feel, would have had the devil's own time with a situation like that.

Hᴏᴍᴇ Fʀᴏɴᴛ ᴀɴᴅ Vᴇʀɴᴀʟ Nᴏᴛᴇs: Cor-
nell has perfected a plant which,
when attacked by insects, bites back. (It is
a variety of mad-dogtooth violet.) A group
of men in Pennsylvania went bear-hunting
the other day with a walkie-talkie set.
They got their bear. Fifty thousand dollars has been raised to stage a fashion show
at the San Francisco peace conference, and
a new board of scientists has been appointed for the development of weapons of war.

↬

It is wonderful news that a Bill of Human
Rights will be submitted at the peace parley. Such a guarantee, however, in order
to be effective, would necessitate a change
in the proposed world-peace structure.
Human rights take shape and meaning
when they are associated with representa-
tive government involving responsibility
and duty. So far, the peace proposals do
not include popular representation in the
council and the assembly, and the people
therefore assume no personal responsibility for anything and therefore will gain no

personal rights. Commissions (stop us if we are wrong about this) cannot create human rights.

Mrs. Roosevelt apparently does not want anyone to write stuff like the paragraph above. In a recent column she expressed the fear that 'perfectionists' would wreck the chances of getting some kind of peace organization through the Senate. 'Those who cannot compromise should be looked down upon by their neighbors,' she wrote. We have been going on the assumption that during the period of the preliminary peace talks, it is a citizen's function to air his opinions and instruct his delegates according to his lights. We intend to go to work on the Senate and urge it to join in world affairs when the Senate itself has something to go to work on. Meantime, we will continue to believe that although a man may have to compromise with Russia he can never compromise with truth. Our neighbors can look down; the top of our head is not much of a sight.

We are a perfectionist to the extent that we regard this world as an imperfect one and consequently in need of the best possible government of law, order, and human rights based on human responsibilities. To us, a perfectionist is someone who wants another man's neighbors to look down on him for having an opinion.

April 14, 1945

As we write this, Russia has just 'denounced' her neutrality pact with Japan. Finishing up a pact of neutrality is like finishing up a pack of cigarettes: you crumple it in your hand, smile, and announce that it has 'lost its meaning.'

❧

You don't have to be an oceanographer to discern strong currents which may deflect the San Francisco conference into new channels. Senator Vandenberg has proposed certain amendments to the Dumbarton Oaks plan, with the intention of injecting two new ingredients — the idea of fluidity and the concept of justice. Neither fluidity nor justice got into our own Constitution by accident, and of course once you begin injecting justice into a political framework you find yourself casting around for a body of law to hang the justice on. Commander Stassen, whose hopes for a world order include basic law, is said to have up his sleeve a suggestion for a constitutional convention to be held at some later date. And the legislatures of thirteen states have passed resolutions approving the principle of federation in world government. These things are disturbing and puzzling to the leaders who are facing the tough, practical details of bringing the nations together and who, being on the inside, know better than the people the consequences of straying from the prearrangements of Dumbarton Oaks. The peace is now in that perilous stage when the very discussion of the theme endangers the friendly relationships the theme is designed to perpetuate.

One thing we can be glad of is that the conference is to be held in this country. The United States is regarded by people everywhere as a dream come true, a sort of world state in miniature. Here dwell the world's emigrants under one law, and the law is: *Thou shalt not push thy neighbor around.* By some curious divinity which in him lies, Man, in this experiment of mixed races and mixed creeds, has turned out more good than bad, more right than wrong, more kind than cruel, and more sinned against than sinning.

This is the world's hope and its chance. The Senator is right — when you have fluidity and justice, the people get on all right.

WALT WHITMAN turned in the ablest report last week and wrote the perfect account of the President's last journey (and the processions long and winding and the flambeaus of the night). It was quite natural that he should have, and it was ingenious of the *World-Telegram* to give him the space he deserved on the front page. Walt's barbaric yawp, his promulging of democracy, his great sweep and love of the people, had been finding political verification during the past dozen years, and when he wrote of the slow and solemn coffin that passes through lanes and streets, through day and night, with the great cloud darkening the land, with the pomp of the inlooped flags, he was simply filing the continuing story of democracy, shoulder to shoulder with the Associated Press.

For a while after the President's death, our thoughts were cool and amorphous — a private phenomenon which often attends grim public occasions. But a day or so later, in line of duty, we found ourself in the council chambers of those to whom

Mr. Roosevelt's death brought a secret sense of relief and the intimations of new life. It was there, by inversion, amid the hopes and yearnings of these people, that we again felt the flame of the President's spirit, for here was the welcoming band, the reception committee, ready to re-embrace the status quo, the special privilege, the society of the white Protestant élite, the clipped hedge that guards the inviolate lawn. Here were the conciliators, their hands outstretched to scratch the ears of all the dragons he had tilted with — injustice, compromise, intolerance. It was no wonder, as we walked home, that Walt's old words seemed a perfect fit for the news, no wonder so many millions were at that moment trembling with the tolling tolling bells' perpetual clang and muttering under their breath, 'Here, coffin that slowly passes, I give you my sprig of lilac.'

It seems to us that the President's death, instead of weakening the structure at San Francisco, will strengthen it. Death almost always reactivates the household in some curious manner, and the death of Franklin Roosevelt recalls and refurnishes the terrible emotions and the bright meaning of the times he brought us through. By the simple fact of dying, he has again attacked in strength. He now personifies, as no one else could, all the American dead — those whose absence we shall soon attempt to justify. The President was always a lover of strategy: he even died strategically, as though he had chosen the right moment to inherit the great legacy of light that Death leaves to the great. He will arrive in San Francisco quite on schedule, and in hundredfold capacity, to inspire the nations that he named United.

Today, tomorrow, or a day not far off, the great wish, the long dream, will come true — the end of war in Europe. There may be no surrender, no last laying down of arms, but the victory will be there just the same, the bloody miracle which once seemed hardly possible will have come to pass. 'You and eleven million other guys,' said the American sergeant to von Papen when he said he wished the war were over. President Roosevelt loved these eleven million other guys very much, and he was well aware that war's end for the soldier in arms would be war's beginning for all the rest of us combined, and for the soldier, too. The President knew this as well as any other man, or better. The guns that spoke in the Hudson Valley last Sunday morning, and Fala's sharp answering bark, were the first salvo of his new fight — for freedom, human rights, peace, and a world under law.

W<small>E READ</small> a little story the other day about the flag that has been designed for the United Nations. It is to be displayed, the story said, 'under' a nation's own flag. Apparently, if you believe in world government, you stand on your head to salute it.[1]

[1] No United Nations flag was displayed in San Francisco, either under or over the flags of the member nations. Question of standing on head never arose.

FINAL VICTORY in Europe came when American and Russian soldiers got drunk together on the Elbe, but it was final in deed only. Final victory came again when the Associated Press could hold life's liquor no longer and spilled it on the town. Still it wasn't final. The bell-man waits beside his bell, the plate-glass window trembles behind its wallboard shield, the citizen paces his hotel bedroom twiddling with his rattle and sampling his bottle of booze. This is the Devil's New Year's Eve, with midnight refusing to come. Final victory came for a third time when Italian patriots poured the last avenging round into Mussolini's back and spat in his dead face. It still isn't final. And when the clock strikes and the bell rings and the word is said and the last blood is squeezed from what Jan Masaryk called 'Hitler's vulgar Valhalla,' even then victory isn't final. Everyone knows that, too. Already the celebrant savors the moment just past midnight, the wearing off of the wine of victory, and thunder in the morning.

It was T. V. Soong, on the afternoon of the second day, who managed to open the United Nations Conference. We were sitting in the peanut gallery of the Opera House, almost asleep after twenty-four hours of platitudes, when Doctor Soong remarked, 'If there is any message that my country . . . wishes to give to this Conference, it is that we are prepared . . . to yield if necessary a part of our sovereignty to the new international organization in the interest of collective security.' Immediately the audience clapped — the first time a speech had been interrupted since the show started. Everyone had been waiting for the sound of life, but it had not come. Various words had been tried by various speakers — by Truman and Stettinius, by the Governor and the Mayor. The word 'unity' had been tried, but it was obvious that we were witnessing not unity but multiplicity. The word 'order' had been tried. But the eye and the ear could find nothing but disorder anywhere in the world. Then Doctor Soong raised his trumpet and blew the word 'sovereignty,' and everybody jumped.

It is an awkward paradox that the first stirrings of internationalism seem to tend toward, rather than away from, nationalism. Almost everything you see and hear in San Francisco is an affirmation of the absolute state, a denial of the world community — the flags, the martial music, the uniforms, the secret parley, the delicate balance, the firm position, the diplomatic retreat. Ninety per cent of the talk is not of how people shall be brought together but of the fascinating details of how they shall be kept apart. And under all is the steady throbbing of the engines: sovereignty, sovereignty, sovereignty.

Statesmen and diplomats are, of course, nationalists both by instinct and by profession. When they are on foreign soil, at a congress, they are doubly cautious and wary. Poets would make better delegates — poets, or barbers, or machinists' helpers, or soldiers. Poets have been singing this stuff for years uncounted, and they are still singing it. We emerged into the city after the first plenary session and found copies of the *News* being hawked on Market Street, with Archie MacLeish's latest song on the front page. Some day people will put faith in poets, who saw things centuries ago in perfect clarity.

＊

We feel unaccountably hopeful that something good will come, not from Dumbarton Oaks but from San Francisco's proliferative power. The Conference began in the midst of deep disturbances and tensions. You could feel them in the roots of your hair. Over the city the Polish question hovered like a foul bird. In the newspapers, in macabre juxtaposition, were pictures of the naked victim of German cruelty and pictures of the well-dressed American platform speaker. Even California itself contributed a tiny blob of darkness to the scene: a group of preservationists (we saw by the papers) were attempting to restrict residence in a certain area to 'people of the Caucasian race.' But although the air was heavily charged with cosmical disturbances, it was not oppressive. It was buoyant and alive. People were shouting that they wanted order and would not accept a spurious document.

Soldiers want it, and they are represented here and they are talking. And it is now a matter of record that the first applause of the United Nations Conference on International Organization was evoked not by the dulcet platitudes of high resolve but by Doctor Soong's tough excursion into cost accounting. As it stands, Dumbarton Oaks won't cost China or any other country one centimeter of sovereignty. But it is an extremely important fact that China thinks it should. We tried some years ago to build a building without a cent of cost to anybody, and look what the people have paid for it recently.

⌐

If we had been Stettinius (and nothing seems more unlikely), we would have opened the meeting with a text from *Walden,* fifteenth chapter, second verse: 'One night in the beginning of winter, before the pond froze over, about nine o'clock, I was startled by the loud honking of a goose, and, stepping to the door, heard the sound of their wings like a tempest in the woods as they flew low over my house.

[83]

They passed over the pond towards Fair-Haven, seemingly deterred from settling by my light, their commodore honking all the while with a regular beat. Suddenly an unmistakable cat-owl from very near me, with the most harsh and tremendous voice I ever heard from any inhabitant of the woods, responded at regular intervals to the goose, as if determined to expose and disgrace this intruder from Hudson's Bay by exhibiting a greater compass and volume of voice . . . It was one of the most thrilling discords I ever heard. And yet, if you had a discriminating ear, there were in it the elements of a concord such as these plains never saw nor heard.'

T HERE'S only one thing you can say for the German war — the men who fought and won it knew, in a general sort of way, what it was all about. Soldiers in the mass are not intellectual giants, but they have a quick grasp of broad meanings. Allied soldiers had a hunch that they disliked the idea behind the word *'Heil.'* They preferred the word 'Hi' — it was shorter and cleaner. It seems beyond belief that the entire globe should have split up over these two words, but if half the world was determined to pit itself against the other half, there couldn't have been a better argument.

The German nation, once great and cultured, today is a poisonous pool of memories and shadows because it presumed to inject the filthy word *'Heil'* into the world. And under so many crosses lie so many kids who can never again say 'Hi.' Last February we remember reading about the capture of Ordensburg-Vogelsang, a school for Führers, by the Ninth Infantry Division of the United States First Army. That school housed the ugly monster of Nazism in pure form, so that German males could pattern themselves upon it. We recall a passage quoted from a pamphlet by Doctor Robert Ley, who occupied a chair in Germany's university of hate. He was explaining that, once you matriculated in Ordensburg-Vogelsang, there was no turning back — you were in for keeps. 'Such are the hard and inexorable laws of the order,' wrote Doctor Ley. 'Every National Socialist leader must know that he is climbing a steep grade. You can walk here only if you have the sleep-walker's sure touch.'

So ended the war against the race of people who wanted to walk straight and far, without the restraints of the senses, as though they had just arisen from bed and walked in perpetual sleep.

~

One thing we notice in San Francisco is how quickly a person becomes a country in the eyes of all. Here, in this international setting, Eden is England, Molotov is Russia, Stettinius is the United States, Soong is China. Because of this illusion, the vast millions of people whose lives and fortunes are bound up in these ticklish negotiations often seem lost in some limbo, and the world narrows to the dimensions of a chessboard and to the visible kings and knights. The earth becomes as quickly diagrammed as when, at a dinner table, you say, 'Here, this salt shaker is the Statue of Liberty, this butter plate is Long Island, this knife is the Hudson River.' Once or twice during the past few days in San Francisco, we have dared to close our eyes and try to remember, as Eden came by, the islands and the ships and the men and the women that are England. We tried to remember, as Soong walked through, the land and the cities and the people that are China — just as you might gaze at the table knife and try to see the Hudson River, the shad fishermen below High Tor, and the waves trembling in the sun.

It is a confusing thing, this phenomenon of personification which turns a statesman into a state. Let him put his arm around another man, and to all appearances you have an alliance. Let him wrinkle his brow, and you have a disturbed condition. Let him say a foolish thing — which any man is likely to do at any moment — and you have a national trend. We recall the stinging letters the Republicans wrote to the papers on that occasion when President Roosevelt's tongue slipped and he referred to 'Russia, Britain, and me.'

A security league must of necessity be founded on two structural misconceptions which endanger the lives of those who will inhabit the building. We mention them not in complaint but as a matter of observation, and because we think the record must at all costs be kept straight in this emergency and at this moment when, again, so much depends on so few. The first misconception is the assumption that nation-states are capable of, or even desirous of, applying law and justice to each other. There is very little historical basis for any such assumption. The second is the belief that peace is a negative matter, to be achieved by preventing aggression.

The expressed objectives of the United

Nations' organization are far in advance of any machinery yet proposed for bringing them to life. This is no secret, either to the delegates or to the many hundreds of hangers-on at this meeting, some of whom are soldiers back from war. The few soldiers we have talked to have been bewildered and skeptical. Words are being used in this conference in a free and easy way. The word 'justice,' the word 'law,' the phrase 'human rights' are being written into the document by those who hope and pray that such words will take hold and mean something. In one sense, it is a good thing that the aims and hopes of people everywhere should be expressed clearly in the charter. In another sense, it is questionable whether any charter should give people the impression that justice and law are inherent in a league of independent sovereign powers, or that human rights can be disassociated from human government.

It would be deluding the people to imply that controversies, from now on, will be settled in accordance with 'principles of justice,' when there is every reason to suppose that they will continue to be settled in accordance with the methods of diplomacy — especially those controversies that greatly matter. This week everyone has watched a couple of major controversies, involving whole populations, settled, quite without recourse to principles of justice or law, simply because the disputes were in the international area, where justice and law do not now operate and will never operate until there is international government.

Here in San Francisco, half the day in fog, half the day in sunshine, are assembled many representatives of minority groups. They are articulate and insistent. To them the rights of man are no joke and no mystery. To them the concept of international justice, decency, and law seems like the last hope for their people. Each sees the problem of peace and of a better world through the lens of his own national or racial problem; each is familiar with the facts of persecution, misery, degradation, and war. These representatives are continually pressing the delegates with sharp questions about human rights. The answer to their questions is always 'We are creating a mechanism.'

It is proper for a league of nations to affirm and praise human rights, but it is dangerous for a league to promise them until it can point to some way by which it can fulfill that tremendous promise. People, not states, create human rights, when they form governments, make laws, sit in courts, and enforce decisions. Up to that point, and short of that point, rights do not come into existence for human beings, and disputes are anarchical and violent, like the last hours of a tyrant, who is outside justice in life and in death. Those who hang the robes of justice around the shoulders of a security organization composed of sovereign independent states do so at their own risk, and at ours. They may easily be endowing that organization with an apparent majesty beyond its political capacity. It is an uneasy occasion, like the conferring of an honorary degree upon a man of no mental breadth by a university which is hard up for cash.

There was one great moment in the war — that was the moment in 1940 when

England suggested that France unite with her and that they become one people, under law. Churchill proposed it, but it slipped away. Things became less desperate and the moment was lost to humanity. We often wonder when the next moment like that will come for the world, and under what hard conditions.

W E HAVEN'T HEARD what, if anything, is being done about finding a name for the new league of nations. The name 'United Nations' will presumably have to be dropped, since the organization is to be an association, not a union, and it is unwise to lead people into believing that they are getting something they aren't. One of the San Francisco papers made an unconscious suggestion for a title the other day when its proofreader was dozing. The paper came out with a reference to 'the Untied Nations,' a far more accurate phrase than the one intended. The work of transposing the 't' and the 'i' now begins in the composing room of time. It may take a long while, but it is worth doing, if only so that the preamble can eventually open with, 'We, the people . . .' instead of 'We, the high contracting powers . . .' [1]

[1] The preamble was revised. It reads, 'We the peoples . . .' With an 's.'

THE *Daily Mirror* has been inquiring around among homemakers, and it reports that the prime desires of the American housewife are: (1) defeat of Japan, (2) economic security for her family in the future, and (3) a new vacuum cleaner.

We have seen the female American dream expressed in many forms, but never so succinctly. National triumph, personal safety, and no dust.

The *Mirror* article went on to project a vision of the future, when our pent-up desires for household appliances and highway vehicles will be loosed upon a reconverted world. The vision was of a vast and expanding national health. It did not particularly impress us, any more than does Doctor de Kruif's picture of the rejuvenated male. The hounds that track the nation's health still sniff a doubtful tree. People will begin to improve their health when they begin seriously to improve their soil, not their sewing machines. It is not our high-octane lawnmower that matters, it is what we do with the grass clippings. (They must be composted and returned to all our gardens.) At home we should decentralize and add organic material to the field. Abroad we should federalize and add organic law to the planet. But instead, we add another bag of chemicals to quicken the young bean vine and a shot of de Kruif's testosterone propionate to brighten the old farmer. We spray our apples and our cabbages with lead poison and take another life-insurance policy to offset the degenerative effect of arsenate upon our kidneys. The delegate from Lebanon was right when, addressing the plenary session, he said, 'There is a security which is utterly insecure.' (French and British papers please copy.) And the Squire of Pleasant Valley is right, too, terracing his Bromfield slopes with the profits from books, and adding dung and leaf mold to Ohio's dirt. Even the Bible, that best-seller, is right, and the house built on a sandy place somehow slips off and goes downhill.

MANY EXCELLENT SITES have been proposed as headquarters for the United Nations, but the location we like best is the Black Hills of South Dakota. Staunch advocacy of this site appears from time to time in the appendix of the *Congressional Record,* and we have been following it, first with interest, lately with enthusiasm. Unquestionably, the seat of the new world league should be Dinosaur Park, near Rapid City, South Dakota, in the Black Hills, for in Dinosaur Park stand the cement figures, full size, of the Big Five of Long Ago — *Tyrannosaurus rex* (35 feet long, 16 feet high), *Triceratops* (27 by 11), *Brontosaurus* (90 feet long, weight 40 tons), and a couple of other plug-uglies of the period, all of them in combative attitudes astride a well-worn path. Much can be said for such a bizarre setting. Here let the new halls be built, so that earnest statesmen, glancing up from their secret instructions from the home office, may gaze out upon the prehistoric sovereigns who kept on fighting one another until they perished from the earth.

THE NAVY feels cramped in Annapolis and wants to buy the St. John's College campus, next door to the Academy. Secretary Forrestal says that acquisition of the thirty-two-acre plot is vital to national security. St. John's says that hanging on to its campus is vital to *its* security. It's a nice dispute. We rather doubt that anybody knows what is vital to national security any more, if indeed anyone ever did. The head of St. John's, Doctor Stringfellow Barr, is one of the people who believe that if the nation is to rest secure the world will have to have a federal government, and we imagine that his views permeate the air of the campus and give it life. This in itself may advance our national security. The Navy, on the other hand, quite naturally believes that national security is in the hands of the U. S. Navy, just as it always has been. Both views appeal to us. After all, there aren't many colleges that have a federalist for a president, and we shouldn't want to see one of them kicked around. And if another war should ever get under way, with mirrors hanging in the sky to turn the sun's rays upon us, our warships might easily be burned to a crisp before the Navy could weigh anchor. Who knows? Not Forrestal. Not Barr. Not us. That being the case, this is no time to evict a college, particularly one like St. John's. It is obvious what we owe the Navy in this war, but it is anybody's guess what we'll owe Doctor Barr if the next war can be prevented.

WE HOPE the Senate will ratify without delay the Charter of the United Nations. We wish the nations had chosen to set up something more businesslike and more costly than a league, but they didn't, and the best this country can do now is join up and start making improvements fast. The principles expressed in the Charter are high. The purposes expressed are good. The preamble begins, 'We the peoples . . . ' The spirit at San Francisco was democratic. Therefore we hope the United States will go in boldly and get wet all over and see what can be done to turn the United Nations into a union that can serve the needs of humanity, for they are great. And on this occasion we recognize the fears expressed by Senator Harlan J. Bushfield in a radio address — fears that membership in the league will place our sovereignty in the hands of 'foreigners.' Every step in the unification process that is going on in the world has aroused just such fears and hesitancies and horrors. Josiah Quincy, congressman from Massachusetts, put it beautifully in 1819, when

Alabama was being admitted to statehood.

'You have no authority,' he said, 'to throw the rights and property of this people into the "hotch-potch" with the wild men on the Missouri, nor with the mixed, though more responsible race of Anglo-Hispan-Gallo-Americans who bask on the sands in the mouth of the Mississippi. . . . Do you suppose the people of the Northern and Atlantic States will, or ought to, look with patience and see Representatives and Senators from the Red River and Missouri pouring themselves upon this and the other floor, managing the concerns of a seaboard fifteen hundred miles, at least, from their residence?'

The wind has been blowing on Capitol Hill for a hundred and twenty-five years, and the words of Josiah Quincy still haunt the conscience of men of good fear. But the planet rolls on. Even as we sit here copying down the 1819 argument of the Gentleman from Massachusetts, one of Missouri's wild men is sitting in a foreign land, in Potsdam, with a wild Englishman and a wild Russian, trying to make the world less hotchy, less potchy, more of a piece.

Dᴏᴡɴ in the cellar in Berchtesgaden, among some straw wine wrappers, a copy of *The New Yorker* was found. It was our issue of September 25, 1937. We have just gone through that back number to see if it contained anything of special interest to the Chief. (It is safe to assume that in the fall of 1937 Hitler was more than a little interested in American folklore.) One rather obvious thing in the issue was a cartoon, by Carl Rose, showing a group of foreign statesmen seated around a conference table, one of the statesmen remarking, 'Oh, let's declare war and get the whole damn thing over with.' It seems possible that Hitler's rat-nosed assistant spotted that one and sent it along marked 'For your information,' or 'What d'ya make of this?'

But a more careful search through the issue has led us to a different conclusion. We believe that if Hitler was studying the magazine at all, it was because of the full-page color ad of World Peaceways, a non-profit organization for public enlightenment on international affairs. That ad, if you recall your 1937, was one of a series. Magazines donated space. Artists and writers donated their services. Peace was what people were groping for, and when Americans grope for something they turn naturally to display advertising and grope all over the place. The peace ad must have given Der Führer confidence to go ahead with his plans — for it is easier to ready one's airways if somebody else is readying his peaceways.

This ad, in particular, was a perfect example of the copywriter's art. It pictured an American suburban scene, with an American homeowner in his shirt sleeves, pipe in mouth, polka-dot tie unruffled, tending his petunias. The caption read, 'The most powerful man in America!' (It even had the standard American punctuation, an exclamation point, in the caption.) The burden of the ad was that the most powerful man in America was Mr. Average Citizen. 'He doesn't want war. He doesn't want to give up his job, leave his wife and youngsters, live like an animal in trenches.' (The word 'foxhole'

[102]

hadn't reached the advertising agencies in September, 1937.)

The decadence, the idiocy of a country in which the most powerful man was Everyman must have given the German leader a lift. In fact, almost everything in the September 25th issue of *The New Yorker* boded well for Germany's future. The ads depicted not only a peace-loving society but a pleasure-loving one as well. Agents for towering apartment buildings were calling softly to tenants: come to 'fashionable Murray Hill,' 'fashionable Sutton Place.' The Sherry-Netherland invited 'leisurely inspection.' The wines were full-bodied, the Scotch was ancient, the milk was irradiated, the wallpaper was Imperial, and the Canadian Pacific was glad to take you round the world via Japan, China, Macassar, Bali, Surabaya, Batavia, Sabang, the Mediterranean, and London. The Rockettes had been abroad and had taken Paris by storm. Furthermore, our Yachting column, in that issue, contained the reverberating news that an owner of a Six Metre boat was seriously considering equipping her with a gold

[103]

keel. If any doubts lingered in Hitler's mind, surely the news that Americans were busy putting golden keels on sailboats was enough to dispel those doubts. America, he might reasonably assume, was in the bag.

But an issue of any American magazine, of whatever date, is not wholly to be trusted as a guide to dictators. Now, eight years later, we feel a certain saucy satisfaction in noting, for our own records, that the man who wrote the Yachting column for our Berchtesgaden issue subsequently commanded an LCI at the beaches of Africa, Sicily, Italy, and Normandy, and was too busy, during those landings, to know whether his keel was gold or dross. There is a moral in it for the would-be conquerors of the future: Never read a magazine on the eve of a great adventure.

W E WERE in the kitchen putting up string beans when the news came that Japan was trying to surrender. It was a warm, bright morning and our little old-fashioned Sears Roebuck Kook-Kwick Canner was boiling cheerfully along under ten pounds' pressure. With a pot holder in each hand, we had settled down for a thirty-five-minute tour of duty, solemnly vowing that whether Japan quit or not we would keep at least one household in the American homeland from blowing up.

Tending a pressure canner is man's work, not because men understand steam gauges any better than women do or because they can endure heat more easily but because a man finds it impossible to keep his hands off anything that seems to call for special knowledge and because he is drawn toward any infernal machine. The radio was going under its own head of steam in the dining room, and two commentators, ad-libbing, were quarreling loudly over the prerogatives of the Emperor. Their voices filled the air and made the kitchen operation seem more desper-

[105]

ate. With our eye glued to the gauge, as we now and again shifted the canner toward or away from the hot part of the stove to keep the pressure from fluctuating, we were thinking how out-of-date we were, canning beans instead of freezing them. Just then a small female relative of ours who was born during the Civil War came through the kitchen and paused to survey the awesome scene with an amused and friendly gaze. 'It's always like this putting things up!' she shouted. 'Preserving always coincides with some great event. I remember making currant jelly one sizzling Fourth of July, giant firecrackers exploding all up and down the block, and the kitchen about a hundred degrees. And now you've got this stove all whooped up while they're trying to finish off Japan with those awful bombs. I never knew it to fail. Human beings don't change. And thank God for that.'

During our vigil with the beans, we thought back over the whole long war, trying to remember the terrible distances and the terrible decisions, the setbacks, the filth and the horror, the bugs, the open wounds, the fellows on the flight decks and on the beaches and in the huts and holes, the resolution and the extra bravery — and all for what? Why, for liberty. 'Liberty, the first of blessings, the aspiration of every human soul . . . every abridgement of it demands an excuse, and the only good excuse is the necessity of preserving it. Whatever tends to preserve this is right, all else is wrong.' And we tried to imagine what it will mean to a soldier, having gone out to fight a war to preserve the world as he knew it, now to return to a world he never dreamt about, a world of atomic designs and portents. Some say this is the beginning of a great time of peace and plenty, because atomic energy is so fearsome no nation will dare unleash it. The argument is fragile. One nation (our own) has already dared take the atom off its leash, has dared crowd its luck, and not for the purpose of conquering the world, merely to preserve liberty.

In England the other day a philosopher and a crystallographer held a debate. The question was whether a halt should be called on science. The discussion was academic, since there is no possibility of doing any such thing. Nevertheless, it was a nice debate. Professor Bernal, the crystallographer, argued that children should be allowed to play with dangerous toys in order that they may learn to use them properly. Joad, the philosopher, said no — science changes our environment faster than we have the ability to adjust ourselves to it.

The words were hardly out of his mouth when a blind girl in Albuquerque, noticing a strange brightness in the room, looked up and said, 'What was that?' A bomb had exploded a hundred and twenty miles away in the New Mexican desert. And people all over the world were soon to be adjusting themselves to their new environment. For the first time in our lives, we can feel the disturbing vibrations of complete human readjustment. Usually the vibrations are so faint as to go unnoticed. This time, they are so strong that even the ending of a war is overshadowed. Today it is not so much the fact of the end of a war which engages us. It is the limitless power of the victor. The quest for a substitute for God ended suddenly. The substitute turned up. And who do you suppose it was? It was man himself, stealing God's stuff.

We have often complained that the political plans for the new world, as shaped by statesmen, are not fantastic enough. We repeat the complaint. The only conceivable way to catch up with atomic energy is with political energy directed to a universal structure. The preparations made at San Francisco for a security league of sovereign nations to prevent aggression now seem like the preparations some little girls might make for a lawn party as a thunderhead gathers just beyond the garden gate. The lemonade will be spiked by lightning. The little girls will be dispersed.

Nuclear energy and foreign policy cannot coexist on the planet. The more deep the secret, the greater the determination of every nation to discover and exploit it. Nuclear energy insists on global government, on law, on order, and on the willingness of the community to take the responsibility for the acts of the individual. And to what end? Why, for liberty, first of blessings. Soldier, we await you, and if the place looks unfamiliar, forgive us. We shall try to restore certain characteristics we all love. Please bear in mind that there is a brightness in the room. Even the blind can detect it.

THE COMICS used to have a safe lead of twenty years over science, but the events of the past few weeks have pressed the comics hard and changed the appearance of the field. Science has swung into the rail position; the tired comics feel the hot whip on their flanks. Even the nomenclature suggests a shift in the race. The latest element to turn up is called plutonium — which is Disney with a touch of mineral water. The word uranium had a mighty sound, a solemn sound, an awful sound. Plutonium is a belly laugh. Plutonium, incidentally, is not known in the stars; the stars are too high-minded. Plutonium is a mouthwash used by Mandrake. Plutonium is just something belonging to the comical race of people who started their first atomic fire under a football stadium.

It will be found, eventually, that just as impurities in water become radioactive from transmuted uranium, impurities in thought become radioactive from transmuted facts and figures lurking in the pitchblende of the mind. We have long suspected that impurities in thought become radioactive. It is a major problem. Fascism, one of the commonest impurities in human thought, is unquestionably radioactive.

WE HAVE MISSED Arthur Brisbane during these past few weeks. He was the
one writer who could have handled the
atom as it deserved. It is a tragic thing to us
that we have had to watch this strange new
energy let loose in the world without Mr.
Brisbane's short, clear paragraphs express-
ing the whole business in terms of the
gorilla.

Brisbane was a great believer in New
York real estate. So far, his theory has not
been disproved. It was challenged the
other day, however, by Louis Bruchiss, an
aerial-armaments expert, who predicted
that New York was all done. In order to
save our civilization, he said, we will have
to go underground with it, out of reach of
the new-type bomb. We mustn't wait but
must go immediately, within the year.
The tall cities will peter out and people
will congregate deep down in vast, sub-
terranean communities beneath mountain
ranges. Men will no longer wonder
whether they are men or mice; they will
wonder whether they are men or moles.

We see that Lord & Taylor have accepted Bruchiss's challenge. Stringing along with Brisbane, they have invested six million dollars in a chunk of Fifth Avenue property between Fifty-second and Fifty-third and are planning to put up a new store, right in the atom's path. They are coming uptown to be near Best. Poor old Murray Hill — the stores are leaving it like rats from a burning ship. The hill is exposed not only to the devastating new forces of science but to the familiar old uptown drift of commerce. 'In planning our new store,' President Hoving said, 'we must think along modern, adult lines. . . . The immature thinking that produced the cataclysm after the last war must not be duplicated.' That's always the problem: to know what is immature, what mature. Whether to dive underground with the armament experts, or just drift up to Fifty-second Street and await the vaporization of steel, nestling alongside R.K.O., Saks, and St. Pat's.

We have been studying Lord & Taylor's plans for the new building and we find that there will be a rooftop landing field and hangar for customers arriving by plane but no mooring masts for dirigibles. It all sounds woefully old-fashioned. Doors will open by old-fashioned photoelectric cells. Old-fashioned television sets will flash information on merchandise throughout the store. Glass walls are being discussed, and other functional things out of a past decade. And our guess is that three-dollar articles will sell for the old-fashioned price of $2.98 and that all the clerks will know how to read and write, will carry pencils, and will pause, in the middle of a transaction, to begin work on a trilogy.

WE HEARD the other day that the war-criminals trials are being held up because the floor of the Nuremberg courtroom is unsafe. We don't doubt this; a great many of Germany's underpinnings have been found to be untrustworthy. But we strongly suspect that the long delay in the war trials has been not so much because there was no solid floor under a certain courtroom as because there was no foundation under the new level of justice with which the victorious nations are now fumbling. Here are a handful of accused individuals of great renown, obviously guilty of rank deeds against society. The job is to make their trial seem legal and orderly and just, when in fact they will have to be tried by makeshift processes and on charges of violating laws that are nonexistent. The Allied peoples naturally want to punish these men as they deserve to be punished, and are determined to do so. In order to do it, they face the queer task of holding an individual responsible for an antisocial act on an international level. To what page of what statute book does the learned judge turn? There isn't any book. There isn't any page. All is virgin parchment — not a mark to go by. Not even a floor under the courtroom.

The chief thing to remember about international law is that it is *not* law and has never worked. Whenever it has been called upon in a crisis, it has cracked and broken. It is not law, being unenforceable. The chief thing to remember about the laws of war is that they aren't law either. They are Queensberry rules, and there is no referee to break up the clinches. But the wonderful thing is that people are now feeling the need of the kind of law that could bring a man like Kurt Daluege to justice. They want the justice to bring him to. The justice is absent. The international government is absent. People are wondering what's the delay.

Nothing that's going on today is more exciting than these Nuremberg trials. They will be more fascinating than reconversion, more significant than atomic energy. We find the idea of them exciting because they are the unconscious expression of the universal desire for a broader legal structure, and hence for a higher social structure. Inherent in these forthcoming trials is a new legal concept: individual responsibility for anti-human, or inhuman, acts. That can mean only one thing — government on a human (rather than a national) basis. If we can begin the construction of such a world, we can soon have the atom eating out of our hand.

It would be a tremendous help if the lawyers and judges entrusted with the trials would state the matter candidly and tack a big ex-post-facto sign over the courtroom door. It would be a help, for instance, if people were to grasp that the trial of a Quisling or a Pétain differs essentially from the trial of a Goering or a Keitel. Quisling stood trial in Norway, on Norwegian law, charged with betraying his country. This was a standard matter of law and order. Goering will stand trial in no man's land, on no man's law, charged with befouling the earth. Only when people catch this distinction will they realize the potentialities of these trials. They are a hint of what may come, of the legal structure of a new world.

TWO THINGS to watch for this week, outside of mermaids, are an aluminum canoe which has been announced by Grumman and which is porcupine-proof, and a new disease called Tissue Starvation, which has been announced by the Miles Laboratories, promoters of One-A-Day vitamins. A woodsman suffering from tissue starvation in an aluminum canoe that is being attacked unsuccessfully by porcupines is our hero of this week — this strangely fleeting week, week of the Flaming Maple, the Tense Relation, the Starved American Tissue, the Hungry European Stomach.

In Wiesbaden, the other day, seven Germans went on trial for the wholesale murder of some slave workers — Poles and Russians, mostly, who had been put to death for reasons which suited Germany at that particular moment. The trial was conducted by United States officers. According to an account we read of it in the *Times,* the defense attorney, an American captain, challenged the legal basis of the trial and quoted *The New Yorker* to support his argument. Thus this magazine, in the minds of some, will appear to be the friend of murderers, the bedfellow of beasts. Despite this difficult rôle, we stick to our story, and for what we hope is a good reason. The two things which seem vital to us at this point are, first, that the criminals rounded up after a war should be promptly punished for their deeds, and, second, that the special procedure for inflicting such punishment should be clearly admitted to be extra-legal and not palmed off on the world as run-of-the-mill justice. For an American court to hang a German who murdered a Russian during a war is completely outside any legal system that we know anything about, and we believe that it is quite important to state this and not try to obscure it.

The need for a broader justice for men, the need for a broader scheme of life than exists today, is great, and the first step toward constructing it is to recognize its absence. These so-called war trials can be magnificent if they can be made to clarify rather than cloud this issue; they will be extremely valuable as precedents if they are presented as a preview of the justice that may some day exist, not as an example of the justice that we have on hand. We are in favor of the higher level of law by which victorious Americans now seek to punish vanquished Germans for murdering captive Russian slaves. We hope the United Nations organization will catch up with the hard-riding lawyers of Wiesbaden, who are way out in front. Nobody, not even victors, should forget that when a man hangs from a tree it doesn't spell justice unless he helped write the law that hanged him.

Pᶠᶜ Hᴇʀʙᴇʀᴛ Wᴇɪɴᴛʀᴀᴜʙ put a pointed question to us in a letter from New Caledonia this morning. 'How's everything going?' he asked sharply. Well, Private Weintraub, in many respects the world at peace bears a striking resemblance to the world at war. In the Netherlands East Indies the Indonesians and Dutch are fighting, using poisoned darts and some borrowed American equipment. In Indo-China the French governor has announced that France is protecting the minority peoples from Annamite imperialism. In Caracas, capital of Venezuela, the revolutionists are fighting the national guard. In Buenos Aires students are fighting the local Nazis. Russia is working on a five-year economic pact with Hungary. And a House Judiciary Subcommittee is trying to decide whether the legal end of the war was August 14, 1945, or September 2, 1945. This last, Weintraub, is one of those knotty questions that keep legislators worn to the bone.

The National Planning Association has endorsed air power as the most effective instrument for preserving world peace. Henry Holt & Company, after rassling with the devil, have published a book called 'The German Talks Back,' thereby saving freedom of speech for America. (It used to be a publisher's job just to decide whether a book was any good or not, but publishing is not so simple any more, Private Weintraub; it involves bigger issues.) Macy's has received a shipment of Veuve Cliquot 1934 and you can buy it for $9.32 per twenty-six-ounce bottle. In Macdougal Alley the gas lamps, which were shut off during the war, are burning again, shedding their small, poetic light on the antique byway. Paramount is filming a picture on such a vast scale that the director uses a walkie-talkie to communicate with his assistants. At a conference in Dublin, New Hampshire, the other day, a group of serious men decided that the world needed some sort of government and should try to organize one. The *Times,* commenting editorially, maintained that the world was not ready for a government. (There is one thing about the *Times;* it knows what the world is ready for. The world, Weintraub, is ready for tomorrow's *Times*.)

Meanwhile, big things are looming on the common man's horizon. In Buffalo a bank is installing a drive-in window so that you can make deposits, or even withdrawals, without getting out of your car. And one day last week a plane appeared above Teterboro, New Jersey, towing a glider; the glider was cut loose and landed, and what do you think was unloaded? Lobsters. Imagine that!

People are shopping these days. The stores are crowded. Buyers are intent but not gay. The news of the atomic bomb came as a terrible shock to everybody, and the easiest way to take your mind off it is to buy things. People are buying new fall handbags, scatter rugs, folding baby carriages, books on the atomic age, germicidal lamps, and things to nibble on while drinking. They feel driven, people do. Napoleon once said, 'I feel myself driven toward an end that I do not know. As soon as I shall have reached it, as soon as I shall have become unnecessary, an atom will suffice to shatter me. Till then, not all the

[124]

forces of mankind can do anything against me.' Napoleon, of course, failed to foresee that some day it would be possible for him to motor up alongside his bank and draw money without getting out of his car. He died believing he would have to get out. There is really no vision, Weintraub.

Great advances in living are being talked of everywhere. Price controls have been lifted on sauerkraut. Pre-salted celery has been successfully grown, and someone is at work on a pumpkin which will contain cinnamon and clove, ready for going into a pie. A Russian has transplanted the heart of one animal into the body of another and set it going. In Maine hunters are saving two days of the gunning season by flying their deer out of the woods in aerial taxis. Sinclair Lewis has written another novel, so good, the publishers say, that the galleys have been sold to M-G-M for two hundred thousand dollars. Four queen bees have been sent by clipper to France to help out with pollinization in the Rhône Valley.

It has been announced that the critical concentration of uranium is one pound. (Half-pound packages of it are harmless.)

What the critical concentration of lethargy is is still anybody's guess, Private Weintraub. It seems that one of the characteristics of atomic energy is that it frightens most those who possess it. The United States, being in the saddle but having not the slightest desire to ride, is far more nervous about the bomb than are the countries that do not yet know the trick and are merely engaged in finding it out. These unatomic countries have something to occupy their hands and their minds, some logical goal. We in America have reached the goal, and nobody knows which way you turn after you have learned how to destroy the world in a single night. It's hard to know, Weintraub — you who fought well and in a great cause.

November 10, 1945

Dᴵˢᴾᴱᴿˢᴱ, ˢᴄᴀᵀᵀᴱᴿ, cries Doctor Ogburn of the University of Chicago. No use going underground, just go away altogether. Drift apart. Break up. Cities are doomed.

But the cities will not be broken up voluntarily by the inhabitants, who will not scatter but will draw closer. City people stay and die, dreaming of cities of old, and of new, greater cities to come. Already a German, with that methodical spirit for which Germans are distinguished, has invented a process for changing rubble into brick, so it doesn't matter any more about cities' being destroyed: not an ounce of rubble need be wasted. You simply add cement, bake in a medium oven, and serve. What if nobody except dead men attends the feast of brick? That's life.

✐

It is in the Classics Library of the University of Chicago, by the way, that Drawer 346 of the index is labeled 'Sophocles to Spam.' Chicago has a way of putting things.

[127]

The only two people we know anything about who have solved the riddle of the atom are a couple of Australians — a fellow named Charlton and a fellow named Olsen. They have thought the thing over, have looked at it from every angle, and have decided to put to sea in a beer barrel.

The day the 1946 Buick models went on display, Albert Einstein, an aged scatterbrain, proposed that the mysteries of atomic energy be committed to a world government. The Buick, with its Fireball engine and new intake manifold, got a bigger play in the *Times* — 14-point type for Buick, 8-point for Einstein — but in spite of the temptation to lose ourself in the new car we read Einstein's statement rather carefully, since it seemed to give support to our own fumbling opinions. It was, as we knew it would be, utterly fantastic. He said that since the Soviet Union does not possess the secret of the bomb, the Soviet Union should be invited to prepare the first draft of a constitutional government. You see? The man is an eccentric.

However, reason prevailed. A day or two later, calmer heads turned up in the pulpit and in the news. Doctor Moldenhawer, of the First Presbyterian Church, said that the way to keep the peace was through national power, and sixteen leading educators made it plain that the bomb should be handed over to the United Nations — with Fireball sovereignty, floating veto power, and an intake manifold like nobody's business.

One of the most pervasive phenomena that ever hit the United States is the hot lunch for school children. It is the warm sun around which American education now seems to revolve. It is clear and plain. It is inescapable. Wherever you go, the hot lunch has got there ahead of you. It has given parents, scholars, pedagogues, demagogues, civic-betterment leaders, and women's clubs something they can grab hold of with vast satisfaction. It is the one thing that has arisen from the educational mêlée which is tangible, sure, universally comprehensible, and on which there is a considerable measure of agreement. In the exact center of every school system, you find the Midday Bowl, nourishing to young and old alike.

The thing is federal in design (it stems from the New Deal) and it has done so much to unify the nation that one wonders whether it doesn't contain the germ of something far greater. Ever since the United Nations charter was drawn, events have served to divide rather than unite people. Nationalism has stiffened rather than relaxed. Even the atom drives us into our corner, where we try to find comfort in secrecy's last stand. However, the United Nations Organization will soon start to function and the members will assemble, and when they do their first concern should be to find something which can excite people's imagination everywhere — a banner around which every person, however simple-minded, can rally. We respectfully suggest, as the No. 1 item on the agenda at the first session of U.N.O., the hot lunch for scholars. In our opinion, it is absolutely airtight.

The Navy's itch to drop an A-bomb takes us right back to a Fourth of July when our equipment included one extremely large cannon cracker. This shining object had been presented to us by a disorderly uncle who liked to turn up at odd times bearing gifts, and who had the know-how. We nursed and tended the huge cracker all through the eve of the Fourth, and the urge to marry the fuse with fire became almost uncontrollable. Our parents were worried, fretful, and increasingly firm. The affair of the unlighted cracker dragged on through the next day until, toward evening, the cracker was turned over to a local patriotic organization for use by experts. Now it's the Navy's turn to suffer. 'Please, Pop!' beg the admirals. 'Please, can't we *now?*' We predict the Navy will fare better than we did. The Navy will get its way, sooner or later. The explosion will take place.

WE HAVE BEGUN the task of collecting
ideas and documents for the United
Nations Organization to go to work on.
The first document we wish to submit is a
passage from a little girl's notebook, since
it is the shortest statement we have read of
the terrors of nationalism, or clubism. It
follows:

THE CLUB

the members of this club are Susie and Donny,
we spy in this club most of the time and also we
make pictures of where we want to spy. Sometimes we draw pictures and play games on the
blackboard, but still we spy most of the time.
We spy mostly when guests come.

WHERE WE SPY AND WHERE WE HIDE

In the living room we hide under the piano
behind the pink chair and also in our club. In
the dining room we hide under the table and in
the kitchen we hide under the sink in the corner. And sometimes we hide in the hall closet
but we dont very much because the guest dont
go there very much.

THE THINGS WE DO IN THIS CLUB

when people walk past the club we roll
marbles at their feet and when someone sits in

the blue chair we hit them on the head. So that is what we do in this club.

Nations are less candid than children, and their state departments have a less good prose style, but the essential structure is there; the spy system, the places to hide, the waiting for the false move on the part of the guest, the fateful blue chair, the sudden marble. There will be no peace in the household while those club members are under that piano.

—

The world, says Wells, is at the end of its tether. 'The end of everything we call life is close at hand,' he writes in his last literary statement, distributed by International News Service. We note, however, that Mr. Wells went to the trouble of taking out a world copyright on his world's-end article. A prophet who was firmly convinced that the jig was up wouldn't feel any need of protecting his rights. We charge Mr. Wells with trying to play doom both ways.

Wells has been a good prophet, as prophets go, and his crystal-gazing is not to be sniffed at. And even lesser prophets, these days, can feel the 'frightful queerness' that he says has come into life. At the risk, however, of seeming to suggest the continuance of life on earth, we must admit that we found the Wells article unconvincing in places. It is not clear yet, at any rate, whether the world is at the end of its tether or whether Wells is merely at the end of his. His description is not so much of the end of life in the world as of the end of his ability to figure life out. The two are not necessarily identical.

Wells is seventy-nine, and it is possible, of course, that he confuses his own terminal sensations with universal twilight, and that his doom is merely a case of mistaken identity. Most writers find the world and themselves practically interchangeable, and in a sense the world dies every time a writer dies, because, if he is any good, he has been wet nurse to humanity during his entire existence and has held earth close around him, like the little obstetrical toad that goes about with a cluster of eggs attached to his legs. We hope Mr. Wells is wrong for once and that man is not the suicide he looks at the moment. Man is unpredictable, despite Mr. Wells' good record. On Monday, man may be hysterical with doom, and on Tuesday you will find him opening the Doomsday Bar & Grill and settling down for another thousand years of terrifying queerness.

Aʟᴍᴀɴᴀᴄ to be hung by the wood box in the kitchen:

Aᴘʀɪʟ 26 — Doctor T. V. Soong addressing the United Nations Conference in San Francisco: 'If there is any message that my country . . . wishes to give to this Conference, it is that we are prepared . . . to yield if necessary a part of our sovereignty to the new international organization in the interest of collective security.'

Jᴜɴᴇ 13 — Emery Reves in *The Anatomy of Peace*: 'As the twentieth-century crisis is a worldwide clash between the social units of sovereign nation-states, the problem of peace in our time is the establishment of a legal order to regulate relations among men, beyond and above the nation-states.'

Aᴜɢᴜꜱᴛ 11 — Dorothy Thompson in her syndicated column: 'A political deduction as logical as the instinct of self-preservation can immediately be drawn from this greatest of all human discoveries: There must be a world state.'

Aᴜɢᴜꜱᴛ 12 — Robert Maynard Hutchins, Chancellor of the University of Chicago, in a broadcast: 'Up to last Monday, I must confess, I didn't have much hope for a world state. I believed that no moral basis for it existed, that we had no world conscience and no sense of world community sufficient to keep a world state together. But the alternatives now seem clear.'

AUGUST 16 — Stephen King-Hall in the *National News-Letter,* London: 'We must not be afraid to admit that world government is no longer an ideal limited as an objective to societies supported by enthusiasts and short of funds. World government has now become a hard-boiled, practical, and urgent necessity.'

AUGUST 18 — Norman Cousins in the *Saturday Review of Literature*: 'Already he [Man] has become a world warrior; it is but one additional step — though a long one — for him to develop a world conscience. . . . He shall have to recognize the flat truth that the greatest obsolescence of all in the Atomic Age is national sovereignty.'

AUGUST 18 — Freda Kirchwey in the *Nation*: 'A new conference of the nations must be assembled to set up a world government.'

AUGUST 27 — Michael Foot, British M.P., in the New York *Post*: 'What is required is a deliberate resignation of sovereignty, at least on this supreme issue [the bomb]. The fundamental fact of San Francisco was, however, that no such concession would be required of any great state.'

AUGUST 30 — Charles G. Bolté in a letter to President Truman: 'We must strive eventually to achieve a world order based on law, governed by representatives responsible to all the people, and guaranteeing the rights of all men.'

SEPTEMBER 1 — Cord Meyer, Jr., in the *Atlantic Monthly*: 'In international society there is no final authority to which the national states must refer their disputes for settlement. . . . We should frankly recognize this lawless condition as anarchy, where brute force is the price of survival. As long as it continues to exist, war is not only possible but inevitable.'

SEPTEMBER 23 — Editorial in the Chicago *Sun*: 'The wiser backers of the San Francisco Charter realized from the beginning that the world organization set up under it was but a stride in an essential direction. Today the harnessing of the atom means that the course must be greatly speeded to world government: government with sovereign powers, to which all individual nations . . . delegate sovereignty over the affairs which require world control.'

OCTOBER 16 — A group of men and women assembled in Dublin, New Hampshire: 'That in place of the present United Nations Organization there must be substituted a World Federal Government with limited but definite and adequate powers to prevent war. . . .That a principal instrument of the World Federal Government must be a World Legislative Assembly.'

OCTOBER 20 — Editorial in the *Saturday Evening Post*: 'We have come to the point where nothing less than world government will suffice to tailor international politics to hitherto-undreamed-of resources of power.'

OCTOBER 22 — Ralph Barton Perry in *One World in the Making*: 'The one world of which we fondly dream is not designed

[139]

to satisfy the exclusive interest of any man or any group. It contains no masters' or servants' quarters. It serves each interest only by serving all interests. It rests on this widest and all-inclusive base, and on nothing else. It is not an idle dream. It is not a mere playful exercise of the imagination but a project to which men are driven by practical necessity.'

NOVEMBER 1 — Professor Albert Einstein in the *Atlantic Monthly*: 'Do I fear the tyranny of a World Government? Of course I do. But I fear still more the coming of another war or wars. Any government is certain to be evil to some extent. But a World Government is preferable to the far greater evil of wars, particularly with their intensified destructiveness.'

NOVEMBER 8 — Captain Harold E. Stassen at the annual dinner of the Academy of Political Science: 'The world needed government on a world level before the atomic bomb. Now it has become an imperative.'

NOVEMBER 22 — Anthony Eden in the House of Commons: 'Every succeeding scientific discovery makes greater nonsense of old-time conceptions of sovereignty.'

NOVEMBER 23 — Mr. Bevin in the House of Commons: 'I feel we are driven relentlessly along this road; we need a new study for the purpose of creating a world assembly elected directly from the people of the world, as a whole. . . . I am willing to sit with anybody, of any party, of any nation, to try to devise a franchise or a constitution — just as other great countries have done — for a world assembly . . .'

NOVEMBER 24 — Doctor J. Robert Oppenheimer in the *Saturday Review of Literature*: 'It is a practical thing to recognize as a common responsibility, wholly incapable of unilateral solution, the completely common peril that atomic weapons constitute for the world, to recognize that only by a community of responsibility is there any hope of meeting that peril.'

DECEMBER 1 — Doctor Richard D. Present in *Free World*: 'The problem is a much broader one than international control of atomic energy; all measures must be taken to prevent another war. Nothing less than world government can accomplish this.'

[141]

W<small>E WALKED HOME</small> in the cold afternoon
past Franklin Simon's windows,
where the children of all nations revolved
steadily in the light. Most of the stores were
concentrating on the gift aspect of the Na-
tivity, displaying frankincense, myrrh, and
bath salts, but Franklin Simon advertised
the Child Himself, along with a proces-
sional of other children of assorted races,
lovely to behold. We stood and watched
passers-by take in this international and
interracial scene, done in terms of child-
hood, and we observed the gleam in the
eyes of colored people as they spotted the
little colored child in with the others.

There hasn't been a Christmas like this
one since the first Christmas — the fear,
the suffering, the awe, the strange new
light that nobody understands yet. All the
traditional characteristics of Christmas are
this year in reverse: instead of the warm
grate and the happy child, in most parts of
the world the cold room and the starveling.
The soldiers of the triumphant armies return to their homes to find a hearty wel-
come but an unfamiliar air of uneasiness,

uncertainty, and constraint. They find, too, that people are groping toward something which still has no name but which keeps turning up — in department-store windows and in every other sort of wistful human display. It is the theme concealed in the victory which the armies of the democracies won in the field, the yet unclaimed triumph: justice among men of all races, a world in which children (of whatever country) are warm and unafraid.

It seems too bad that men are preparing to blow the earth to pieces just as they have got their hands on a really first-rate idea. Our Christmas greetings this year are directed to the men and women who will represent the people of the world at the meeting of the United Nations Organization in January. We send them best wishes and a remembrance of that first Christmas. Our hope is that they will shed the old robes which have adorned dignitaries for centuries and put on the new cloth that fits one man as well as another, no matter where he lives on this worried and all too shatterable earth.

M AKE AN ORIGINAL and four copies, Miss
Eberhard, one for each delegate. A
delegate, on his way to assembly, carries
two sets of instructions: one dictated by
his own conscience (but not read) and one
handed him by his constituents. Herewith
we hand to each delegate to the first assembly of the United Nations Organization
his instructions:

When you sit down, sit down as an
American if it makes you feel comfortable,
but when you rise to speak, get up like a
man anywhere.

Do not bring home any bacon; it will
have turned rancid on the journey. Bring
instead home a silken thread, by which
you may find your way back.

Bear in mind always that foreign policy is domestic policy with its hat on. The
purpose of the meeting, although not so
stated anywhere, is to replace policy with
law, and to make common cause.

Make common cause.

Think not to represent us by safeguard-
ing our interests. Represent us by perceiv-

ing that our interests are other people's, and theirs ours.

When you think with longing of the place where you were born, remember that the sun leaves it daily to go somewhere else. When you think with love of America, think of the impurity of its bloodlines and of how no American ever won a prize in a dog show.

Carry good men with you in your portfolio, along with the order of the day. Read the men with the short first names: Walt Whitman, John Donne, Manny Kant, Abe Lincoln, Tom Paine, Al Einstein. Read them and weep. Then read them again, without tears.

If you would speak up for us, do not speak up for America, speak up for people, for the free man. We are not dispatching you to build national greatness. Unless you understand this, and believe it, you might better be at the race track, where you can have a good time simply by guessing wrong.

Never forget that the nature of peace is commonly misstated. Peace is not to be had by preventing aggression, for it is always too late for that. Peace is to be had when people's antagonisms and antipathies are subject to the discipline of law and the decency of government.

Do not try to save the world by loving thy neighbor; it will only make him nervous. Save the world by respecting thy neighbor's rights under law and insisting that he respects yours (under the same law). In short, save the world.

Observe that Chapter IV, Article II, Paragraph 3 of the Charter asks the General Assembly to 'call the attention of the Security Council to situations which are likely to endanger international peace and security.' We instruct you, accordingly, to call the Council's attention to the one situation which most consistently endangers peace: absolute national sovereignty. Remind the Council of the frailty, the insubstantiality, of your own Organization, in which members are not people but states.

Do not be confused by the noise of the atomic bomb. The bomb is the pea shooter come home to roost. But when you dream, dream of essential matters, of mass-energy relationships, of man-man relationships. The scientists have outdreamed you, little delegate, so dream well.

Be concerned with principles, not with results. We do not ask for results, merely for a soil-building program. You are not at a chess game, even though it has the appearance of one; you are at a carnival of hope.

For bedside reading we prescribe the opening remarks of Justice Jackson at the Nuremberg trial: 'The idea that a State, any more than a corporation, commits crimes is a fiction. Crimes always are committed only by persons.' (Yet the U.N.O. has been chartered to stop states from committing crimes.) And further: ' . . . that fictional being, "the State," which cannot be produced for trial, cannot plead, cannot testify, and cannot be sentenced.' We instruct you to compare these words with Chapter II of the Charter, which says that the members of your Organization are states. If, as Justice Jackson points out, your membership is a fiction, then your first task should be to become more factual, less fictional. Your task will be to introduce people into the pie. Eventually you will have to supplant states with people, policy with law, diplomacy with legality, internationalism with federal union, and you probably haven't as much time as you like to think you have.

As talisman, do not carry a colored flag for the special occasion; carry a white handkerchief for the common cold. Blow your nose frequently and listen to the universal sound.

Finally, now that the Emperor has disclaimed divinity, we charge you to believe in yourself and to love truth. Build the great republic. The foundation is inescapable. The foundation is unity. It is what your initials suggest: UNO.

AT THEIR earliest convenience the delegates to the United Nations Organization should form an orchestra. There must be, among those seven hundred men and women, enough fiddlers, flautists, cellists, trombonists, and drummers to make up a sizable band, and if the delegates were to organize one, and perform together, the effect on the world would be incalculable. Eleanor Roosevelt could learn the triangle. Once a week all deliberations, all matters of state, should be put aside and the public invited to the assembly hall to hear that rarest of sounds — the concord of nations. Next morning the papers, instead of carrying the latest installment in the long, uneasy story of international dissension, could report that the second movement had never been more solidly handled by the strings and that Vishinsky turned in a masterful performance on the glockenspiel.

There is, in fact, great need that the U.N.O. delegates find some human activity or pastime which will illustrate people's ability to lose themselves in a universal theme, to harmonize, and to create beauty by following a single score rather than fifty-one separate scores. Most of the activities and pronouncements of the delegates in an international arena tend to distort and misstate the relationships of the peoples they represent. In a league, each delegate personifies his country. Whatever happens to him seems, by some preposterous extension, to have happened to all his countrymen. On the first day of the U.N.O.'s meeting in London, a week or two ago, there was the usual jockeying for position, and next morning the papers made us feel that we had personally been in a violent cosmic scuffle with millions of British, Russians, Belgians, Norwegians, and Poles. Yet we had gone through the day, we remembered, without scuffling with anybody at all, and we resented the implication that our day had been otherwise. That is why the delegates (who are professionally preoccupied with trouble, by virtue of their job) should form an orchestra. Imagine a Gershwin morning in the assembly hall, with an all-world symphony group playing music written by an

American of Russian-Jewish extraction about Negroes whose ancestors had come from Africa in slave ships! Imagine 'Summertime' (a universal theme, understandable everywhere) interpreted by Spaak's Revellers!

THE U.N.O. is receiving petitions these days asking that Argentina be suspended because it is 'an enemy of peace and security.' Such a proposal certainly gives one pause. It is a little like recommending that the jackal be turned loose from the zoo because of its smell. Just where the jackal would go on being dismissed, just how it would spend its time if relieved of membership, is, of course, not quite clear. You don't necessarily get rid of a smell by the simple act of refusing to sit in the same room with it. And you do not achieve security by suspending, from a security league, an enemy of security.

The case of Argentina is probably the most instructive and important of any that have arisen thus far. When Argentina landed in San Francisco last spring, the infant league shook from head to toe. To admit Argentina seemed silly. But to refuse to admit Argentina seemed equally queer. The problem quickly showed itself to be not so much the dubious domestic behavior of Argentina as the dubious function of a league of peace-loving nations. In the name of all that is peaceable, should a totalitarian country be inside or outside a security league? Nobody knew then. Nobody knows now.

From a dictator's point of view, there is a certain advantage in having one's country represented in an international organization, provided the organization is simply a league held together with promises. Hitler always said that it was advisable to keep up your membership in such bodies, and keep up appearances, because then you had a better chance to play your own game without being noticed or suspected. It really all simmers down to a matter of design. Under the U.N.O. structure, it is hard to see whether security is served by co-operating with Argentina or by suspending Argentina.

Britain's Mr. Bevin, in what may some day be regarded as the most revolutionary speech of the century, questioned the design of the United Nations on November 23rd last, when he said he'd be glad to sit with anybody, of any party, of any nation, to talk about world government. His offer was not accepted. The Russians and the

Americans looked the other way. One of the Russians remarked that we must stick to the letter of the Charter and not rock the boat. He said that it is the 'spirit,' not the design, that counts. We wonder if he is right. If we were about to step out of a plane and were offered the choice of a parachute or a chest of drawers, we would choose the parachute, on the score of its design.

I<small>T</small> <small>TOOK</small> a Westchester County real-estate deal to get Americans really worked up about the U.N.O. The realization that American homes were actually involved in the thing came as a great surprise. 'It ain't democratic!' shouted a citizen of North Castle, hurling in three words the most constructive criticism that has yet been aimed at the new organization. The people of Westchester, peace-loving by nature, had a feeling they hadn't been consulted in a matter that concerned them closely. The fact that they aren't being consulted in certain other U.N.O. matters — matters on which hangs the fate of every home in every land — has probably not even yet occurred to many. But it will in time, as the debates in the Security Council become increasingly violent and the shadow of the veto lengthens on the living-room rug. If Westchester people want a voice in the world's town meeting, they should take a look at their Charter and start figuring out how they, or anybody else, are going to get one. We urge them to do just this. We urge Iranians to do it, Indonesians, Greeks, British, Russians, Poles. We urge it in Patagonia and in Paterson, New Jersey. We urge people everywhere to make sure that under the Charter they can always know the facts and be consulted. Look to the Charter, everybody, while you still have a home!

A question that keeps bobbing up is whether it is feasible to establish a world capital until you have a world government. This question, indirectly, bothered some Westchester people, too. One of them wrote the *Times* questioning the whole idea of bringing furriners here to our midst. It's a better question than it seems, on the face of it. It is a question to which a group of young federalists, believers in government, have been addressing their minds over the past weekend in Concord, Massachusetts. In our opinion there is no place for furriners in a world capital. Unless the capital of the world houses fellow-citizens, it is not a capital, it is a cave of the winds.

IT WOULD APPEAR that Russia has been spying on Canada — a bit of news which seemed to come as a surprise to everybody. We heard one commentator say that the spy story in Canada was 'as good as a mystery thriller.' We didn't think it was anywhere near as good as a mystery thriller. If there is one thing which no longer should remain mysterious to anyone, or thrilling, it is that every nation must of necessity spy on every other nation. How else can a nation get information which it needs concerning the habits, plans, and secrets of other nations? Spying is not a mystery. To us it is far from thrilling; it is putrefactive.

As a child we played a game called I Spy. As a man, we are fully aware that we live in a society which plays that game, for its life. It plays it because it has always played it and because it hasn't worked out the rules of any other game. Every year the stakes grow higher, the game grows rougher. Soon the barn will fall on the children. If Americans and Canadians grow indignant at Russia for stealing atomic information, they are being innocent beyond belief. If the United States is not at this moment spying on fifty or sixty other nations, to find out what is going on inside their borders, then it is not only innocent, it is derelict. If fifty or sixty other nations are not operating inside the United States, then those other nations are derelict, too. A nation that doesn't spy today is not giving its people an even break.

If there is any sentiment among people generally to abandon the spy system and get on to something forthright, we recommend that they instruct their U.N.O. delegates to get busy on the project. At the moment we are headed not toward but away from it — strengthening national lines and turning global problems over to commissions. Atomic energy will never be controlled by commission. Human rights will never be established by commission. A free press and the right to know will never become universal by commission. Peace is expensive, and so are human rights and civil liberties; they have a price, and we the peoples have not yet offered to pay it. Instead we are trying to furnish our globe with these precious ornaments the cheap way, holding our sovereignty cautiously in one fist while extending the other hand in a gesture of co-operation. In the long run this will prove the hard way, the violent way. The United Nations Organization, which in its present form is a league of disunited nations whose problems are on the table and whose spies are behind the arras, is our last chance to substitute order for disorder, government for anarchy, knowledge for espionage. We better make it good. Remember, an intelligence service is, in fact, a stupidity service; if we were really intelligent, we wouldn't be willing to stake our children's lives on our country's spies.

THE NATIVES on Bikini are being moved to another atoll to make *Lebensraum* for our scientists on Chain Reaction Day. The account we saw of the eviction said that these Bikini Islanders were an unusual bunch — they lived in peace and didn't murder one another. Such people, afflicted with an unnatural lassitude, are out of luck on this up-and-coming planet and it is not surprising that they are having to move on. Presumably nothing much will be left of Bikini when the scientists get through; it will simply be remembered as the one-time habitation of some queer dicks who failed to drop things on each other.

Two hundred goats, two hundred pigs, an undetermined number of sheep, and thirty-seven hundred rats have been assigned the best seats for the Bikini show. They are going to be placed aboard the target ships. We would like to volunteer to join this plucky crew, as it seems only right that the human race be represented on so vivid an occasion. As yet it has not been definitely established that an atomic bomb can kill a man if he is standing on the deck of a ship. And until we know that, how can anybody rest easy?

Before signing on, however, we would like to examine the Committee's permit to drop the new, improved A-bomb, which, as one scientist put it, 'will cause almost unbelievable damage.' We feel that the papers of a bomb dropper should be in order, and it isn't clear wherein the authority lies for unpredictable detonation. Who issues the permit to blow the fishes out of the sea? What bureau of licenses places its blessing on Nuclear Man, who doesn't know his own strength?

Bikini Lagoon, although we have never seen it, begins to seem like the one place in all the world we cannot spare; it grows increasingly valuable in our eyes — the lagoon, the low-lying atoll, the steady wind from the east, the palms in the wind, the quiet natives who live without violence. It all seems unspeakably precious, like a lovely child stricken with a fatal disease.

There is one more passenger that ought to be aboard a Navy ship on the great day, alongside the goats, the pigs, the sheep, the rats, and us. We think archy ought to be aboard, archy s lineage is truly ancient; he goes back one hundred million years. We've been reading about cockroaches in a book by Edwin Way Teale and we are of the opinion that the cockroach is the creature most likely to survive the atomic age. Sensitive to light and shade, he instinctively seeks the dark (and there should be plenty of that). Furthermore, archy can get along for two weeks without nitrogen, can last many hours without oxygen, and can digest the gold lettering on books.

It will tickle archy to learn that among the persons mentioned to head the Chain Reaction Day Commission is Franklin D'Olier, president of the Prudential Life Insurance Company. One of the maxims archy left in the boss's typewriter one morning was this:

> live so that you
> can stick out your tongue
> at the insurance
> doctor
>
> if you will drink
> hair restorer follow
> every dram with some

                    good standard
                    depilatory
                    as a chaser

Well, archy s boss is dead, God rest his
untransmigrated soul, but archy himself
is probably good for another hundred million years. There will be enough gold lettering from pulverized books to keep him
going, and, as we pointed out, his nitrogen
needs are small. Because he had the soul
of a poet and saw things from the under
side, archy s writings are pertinent today,
as the cosmos slithers drunkenly into its
Bikini Lagoon phase. One of archy s ac-
quaintances, you will recall, was a toad
named warty bliggens, who was convinced
that toadstools had been especially created
for him, planned for his personal shelter:

                a little more
                conversation revealed
                that warty bliggens
                considers himself to be
                the center of the said
                universe
                the earth exists
                to grow toadstools for him
                to sit under
                the sun to give him light

by day and the moon
and wheeling constellations
to make beautiful
the night for the sake of
warty bliggens

archy asked him what he had ever done to
deserve such favors from the Creator of
the universe.

ask rather
said warty bliggens
what the universe
has done to deserve me

IN WASHINGTON, as we write this, men are trying to decide whether to present the Iranian matter to the Security Council as a 'dispute' or as a 'situation.'

The question that should be stirring in everyone's mind, including the minds of those men who will sit in the Hunter gym in the name of humanity, is not whether we are dealing with a situation or a dispute; the question is whether we have created the machinery for resolving even the slightest of the world's innumerable difficulties. If we have not, then that is the crisis that should absorb our attention, not Iran. The U.N.O. is the only constituted group which is on the top level. The London sessions did not increase people's confidence. Delegates tried to settle, by accusation and resolution, what in the long run can be settled only through law and justice. Since the London meetings, nations have made private arrangements among themselves, and this has not increased people's confidence. Statesmen are urging people to place their trust and their support in the U.N.O. People would like to. In our opinion, the people's trust and allegiance will be transferred to the U.N.O. the minute the U.N.O. reconstitutes itself as a functioning government, representing the people. Until that moment, the people's trust will be where for centuries it has been, where it traditionally lies, and where it emotionally adheres — in their national governments.

By tuning to WNYC, citizens can listen to the proceedings in the Hunter gym. As in basketball, each person's sympathy will be with his team. Americans will listen to find out how America is doing, Britons will follow England's progress, Russians will cheer when one of their boys shoots a basket. To achieve world order, we must have an over-all government, to which authority is transferred, so that when you tune in on the proceedings, you will root not for which nation you think is right but for which idea you think is right. Supreme Court Justice Douglas said the other day: 'There is a great difference between a world government that represents the peoples of the world and one that represents the nations of the world. . . . Our goal should be a world government representing the peoples of the world, functioning under an international bill of rights, through a legislative, judiciary, and executive.'

Tune in, if you get a chance, and listen to the ball game.

IT MIGHT WELL be recalled at this moment that Gulliver, that traveler,
offered the King of Brobdingnag the secret
of an amazing powder that 'would not only
destroy whole ranks of an army at once
but batter the strongest walls to the
ground, sink down ships, with a thousand
men in each . . . rip up the pavements, tear
the houses to pieces . . . dashing out the
brains of all who came near . . . destroy the
whole metropolis.' The King, struck with
horror that anyone could entertain such
inhuman ideas, said that some evil genius,
enemy to mankind, must have been the
first contriver. 'As for himself, he pro-
tested that although few things delighted
him so much as new discoveries in art or in
nature, yet he would rather lose half his
kingdom than be privy to such a secret,
which he commanded me, as I valued my
life, never to mention any more.'

April 13, 1946

'THE SECURITY COUNCIL shall consist of eleven members of the United Nations.'

A man must have some reading matter with him in the subway. But the I.R.T. is distracting in the early morning. The prettiest girls in the world ride the subway at ten of nine. They ride proudly and with shining hair, as though entered in the lists at Camelot. They are employed and they are newly washed and they do not know (although they're quite ripe to be told) that the Security Council 'shall be so organized as to be able to function continuously' (Article 28).

We were bound north for a crisis meeting of the Council, scheduled for eleven. It struck us, as we put our nickel in, that no crisis worthy of the name can possibly occur at exactly eleven o'clock in the morning. Eleven is too soft and luxurious an hour, too accommodating to the habits of delegates, to be critical. Crises, real ones, must occur earlier than eleven (say at seven-twenty, before a nation has shaved) or much later than eleven (say at nine-two in the evening, after dinner, when a nation is a little drunk). However, an eleven o'clock crisis was our destination and we felt that we had nothing to say about the timing of such things. ('Decisions of the Security Council on procedural matters shall be made by an affirmative vote of seven members.')

Aboard the Woodlawn express we opened our newspaper and read a sober and penetrating column on spheres of influence. The article explained what was going on in the world, and the shape of things to come. It all made a great deal of sense. To put an even finer point on it, it made no sense at all, the author having erred in his count. (There is only one sphere of influence today, and we live on it. It is the sphere on which the Security Council may, at any stage of a dispute of the nature referred to in Article 33, recommend appropriate procedures or methods of adjustment.)

At Bedford Park Boulevard we detrained. The upper Bronx seemed quiet and relaxed. Most of the passengers had left the train before it reached the capital of the world (they had nearer errands,

From a window on the stair landing we looked out at the flags of all nations set up, equidistant, around the big grass circle. The bright sovereignty, the gay equality. And in the center, towering above all, the tall flagstaff without a flag. It seemed dangerously bare. Somebody, we thought, should seize the halyard and run up a token banner to symbolize the world community, even if it were only a pair of scanties. A few minutes after eleven the delegates marched in and took their places, all but one. The ten delegates, the one empty chair. (See Article 28: 'Each member of the Security Council shall . . . be represented at all times at the seat of the organization.' Question of the meaning of the word 'seat,' probably. Matter of interpretation.)

In the back row of the orchestra sat a group of wounded veterans. One of them held crutches that were upholstered in red (color of blood). A few rows further down was a little girl in a yellow sweater and yellow hair ribbon (color of spring). At the stenographers' table, among the verbatim reporters, was a Negro girl (color of tolerance, trouble, human rights). And in the end place of the high tribunal, the unoccupied chair of the Union of Soviet Socialist Republics, empty and green (color of budding organisms).

Sitting there among the press, wearing the wonderful look of infinite understanding that the press wears so well, we stared idly at the empty chair and tried to conjure up the hundred and ninety million people who were (were not) represented by one vacant seat. (We learned from Brooks Atkinson's dispatch in the *Times* next morning that there had been no mention in the Moscow press of the United Nations meeting. As far as the hundred and ninety million people were concerned, the chair was not only empty, it was virtually nonexistent.) The U.N. is not a government, of course, and therefore its chairs at the Council table can be either empty or filled, at the whim of the sitter. (The prime difference between a league of nations and a government of people is that a nation pays its delegate to stay in his chair or leave it according to whether staying or leaving seems to be in the best interests of the nation, whereas a government of people pays its representatives to stick around under all circumstances, on the theory that if a man leaves the room, he not only is betraying the citizens but isn't earning his money.) We rather doubted, thinking about it, that the world community would function satisfactorily as a community in the interests of people as long as it was limited to the concept of salvation by resolution, and with the fifty-one bright flags planted evenly around the circle. There is no compromise, really, between government and non-government. No safe middle ground. The middle ground looks alluring, because it is close at hand, well groomed, and cheap; but it must eventually be crossed. We are in mid-passage today, a tricky moment in time.

Doctor Quo read a letter from Iran and a letter from Russia. Mr. Byrnes addressed the Iranian Ambassador. 'In the light of . . . have you any suggestion as to . . .?' The meeting adjourned, to give everyone time to study the letters.

On the subway again, making the long

post-crisis journey downtown, we bought a *World-Telegram*. 'TENSION EASES,' said the headline. Less tense, we turned to 'News Outside the Door': 'When Jack-in-the-Pulpit, the woodland preacher, comes up from beds of black loam along Troublesome Brook in Westchester in April . . .' The crisis had passed. There wouldn't be another one till eleven o'clock tomorrow. Jack-in-the-Pulpit had appeared by Troublesome Brook.

IN THE SUNDAY *Times* of April 7th there was a letter from a Yale physics professor pointing out that an atomic explosion in the Pacific might open up a hole in the floor of the sea. In that event, wrote the professor, sea water might be forced into the superheated interior of the earth, creating a chain of explosions which would 'transcend the imagination of most human beings' and possibly produce a tidal wave a mile high, overwhelming the inhabitants of Seattle, Portland, San Francisco, Berkeley, Oakland, Los Angeles, and San Diego. The letter also pointed out that another possible effect of the Bikini test would be somewhat more disastrous and fundamental. Submarine explosions (caused by sea water rushing into the earth's bowels) might remove a large mass of material from the equatorial regions and thus might decrease the rotational inertia of the earth itself. 'This,' said the professor, 'would mean a decrease in the length of the day, with the corresponding rise in tempo of many human activities, if any still persisted.'

[177]

The thing that seemed noteworthy about this forecast was that the *Times* ran it on page 10 of the fourth section, and under the head 'Bomb Site Discussed.' Doom (or an intimation of same) is no longer front-page stuff. Too trite.

THEY SAY that when the bombs explode
over Bikini, the heat will equal the interior heat of stars. This is of the utmost
interest to scientists, every one of whom
owes his existence to the earth's having
cooled off.

↞

It is discouraging that at the highest
council table, the conversations should be
on a low level. We sat through a three-
hour debate on whether the Iranian matter should, or should not, remain on the
agenda. It hardly seemed worth debating.
Trouble is always on the world's agenda,
and cannot be dislodged by the vote of
eleven men. Everybody in the room knew
that, and wished it weren't so.

Another long debate was on the question whether Franco's Spain was a threat
to peace. It seemed a senseless argument.
The presence of Fascism anywhere constitutes a threat to peace, and you do not
need to debate it. Fascism enjoys at the
moment an almost perfect climate for
growth — a world of fear and hunger and

[179]

a new, quick weapon of mass destruction which bypasses armies and navies and goes right to the root of the thing, right to the people in their homes in the cities. If the triumphant democracies hope to beat Fascism at its own game, they will have to bypass the academic debates on whether Franco constitutes a threat to peace and whether Iran should be on or off the agenda, and go right to the guts of peace itself — in short, right to the heart of sovereignty. They ducked it at Yalta, they ducked it at Dumbarton Oaks, they ducked it at San Francisco, and now it dogs them relentlessly, and will continue to dog them until they turn and face it.

It has seemed to us that Mr. Gromyko's behavior throughout has been consistent with the letter of the Charter. The Western nations, on the other hand, have been wistfully trying to breathe something into the Council which is not there. The Charter at least has the virtue of candor: it expressly affirms its own impotence. But despite this, the people devoutly wish for a strong implement to translate their high purpose into good results. To us the memorable thing about the United Nations meetings, both in San Francisco, where they were in the foetal stage, and latterly in the Bronx, where they are in infancy, is how desperately people want a world order and how willing they are to invest the new organism with the authority without which it can never properly function.

THE EGYPTIAN DELEGATE, retiring from his presidency of the Council, stepped down in a burst of candor. Doctor Afifi Pasha said he was depressed and humanity was disappointed. It seemed to him nations were acting each to further its own interests, not to further the cause of people generally.

That is precisely the case. To change it around is precisely the task. How set nations to work furthering the universal (rather than the special) cause? What treatment is there for the disease of nationalism, a more troublesome disease at this point than cancer? The treatment is known, but not admired. There is a specific for nationalism. We use it every day in our own localities. The specific is government — that is, law; that is, codification of people's moral desires, together with enforcement of the law for common weal. The specific comes in a bottle and is very expensive. The price is terrific — like radium, only worse. The price is one ounce of pure sovereignty. Too expensive, say the elders of the tribe.

Read the papers and see what the people want. Security. Human rights. Freedom of the press. Peace. Control of atomic energy. Read the papers and see how the statesmen propose to get these plums. Through national power. Through balance of same. Through international accord. Through pacts and agreements (there is the five-year treaty with no frosting, the ten-year treaty with jelly filling, and the twenty-five-year treaty with a prize hidden in the batter). Through commissions. Through Operation Crossroads — to determine which is the more durable, a battleship or a tropical fish. Through foreign policy. Through secret diplomacy (which is merely a redundant phrase for diplomacy). Through the creaky, treacherous machinery of international relations against the same broad, chaotic backdrop of pride, fear, absolute sovereignty, power, and the colorful banners we saluted in assembly hall as pupils in grammar school.

Doctor Afifi is right; the people are not satisfied. During the first post-bellum year, nations have approached the future each to gain its own end. A fair question is this: Can nations now act in any other than a selfish way, even if they want to, given the political equipment which they have provided for themselves? We doubt it. A wrong turn was made somewhere, as far back as the Atlantic Charter — that beloved document which expresses people's desires and their noble aims. The Charter could have shaken the world, but it failed to. It almost made the grade and not quite. It specifically stated the freedoms we grope toward, specifically denied us the means of achieving them. It reserved for each nation full and unlimited sovereignty — and in so doing wrote itself into history's wastebasket. Again, at Dumbarton Oaks, the right turn was avoided, discreetly, and with many words of cheer, of good will.

But the earth, scratching its statesmen as though they were fleas, heaves and rocks with big new things. This is one of those times. The people feel the disturbance. They know it's here, they fear its consequences, and they live in fear. Living in fear, they act with suspicion, with tension. If anyone were to run out into the Square and shout, 'Go east!,' like the characters in the Thurber story, there is a good chance you would see an eastward movement in the panicky noontime; Orson Welles managed it in a mere radio dramatization, way back in the days before the atom was fairly split.

World government is an appalling prospect. Many people have not comprehended it (or distinguished it from world organization). Many others, who have comprehended it, find it preposterous or unattainable in a turbulent and illiterate world where nations and economies conflict daily in many ways. Certainly the world is not ready for government on a planetary scale. In our opinion, it will never be ready. The test is whether the people will chance it anyway — like children who hear the familiar cry, 'Coming, whether ready or not!' At a Federalist convention the other day, Dean Katz of the University of Chicago said, 'Constitutions have never awaited the achievement of trust and a matured sense of community; they have been born of conflicts between groups which have found a basis for union in spite of deep suspicions and distrusts.'

The only condition more appalling, less practical, than world government is the lack of it in this atomic age. Most of the scientists who produced the bomb admit that. Nationalism and the split atom cannot coexist in the planet.

Leadership is the thing, really. And we seem not to have it, anywhere in the world. Premier Stalin's speeches have been strictly jingo since the end of the war. President Truman carries a clipping about the 'parliament of man' in his wallet, and keeps his pocket buttoned. It takes a small country like Egypt even to speak the dissenting words. The large countries speak more cautiously and circle around each other like dogs that haven't been introduced, sniffing each other's behinds and keeping their hackles at alert. The whole business of the bomb tests at Bikini is a shocking bit of hackle-raising, which is almost enough in itself to start a bitter fight in the crazy arena of amorphous fear. One scientist remarked the other day that the chances of the explosion's doing some irreparable damage to the world were one in a hundred septillion. Very good. And if there is one such chance, who can authorize the show? What is the name of the fabulous ringmaster who can play with the earth and announce the odds? There is no such character. The natives who were tossed off Bikini are the most distinguished set of displaced persons in the world, because they symbolize the displacement that will follow the use of atomic power for military purposes. If one atomic bomb goes off, in real earnest, the rest of us will leave our Bikinis for fair — some in the heat of stars, some in the remains of human flesh in a ruined earth.

Government is the thing. Law is the thing. Not brotherhood, not international co-operation, not security councils that can stop war only by waging it. Where do human rights arise, anyway? In the sun, in the moon, in the daily paper, in the conscientious heart? They arise in responsible government. Where does security lie, anyway — security against the thief, the murderer, the footpad? In brotherly love? Not at all. It lies in government. Where does control lie — control of smoking in the theater, of nuclear energy in the planet?

Control lies in government, because government is people. Where there are no laws, there is no law enforcement. Where there are no courts, there is no justice.

A large part of the world is illiterate. Most of the people have a skin color different from the pink we are familiar with. Perhaps government is impossible to achieve in a globe preponderantly ignorant, preponderantly 'foreign,' with no common language, no common ground except music and childbirth and death and taxes. Nobody can say that government will work. All one can guess is that it must be given an honest try, otherwise our science will have won the day, and the people can retire from the field, to lie down with the dinosaur and the heath hen — who didn't belong here either, apparently.